BOB MATHIAS

The Life of the Olympic Champion

BOB MATHIAS

The Life of the Olympic Champion

FOREWORD BY BRUCE JENNER/AFTERWORD BY BOB MATHIAS
BY MYRON TASSIN

Produced with a grant from the Southland Corporation, a corporate sponsor of the 1984 Summer Olympics

St. Martin's Press
New York

Design by R. Knots

Library of Congress Cataloging in Publication Data

Tassin, Myron.
  Bob Mathias : the life of the Olympic champion.

  1. Mathias, Bob, 1930– . 2. Athletes--United
States--Biography. I. Title.
GV697.M3T37 1984 796.4′2′0924 [B]   83-21194
ISBN 0-312-08730-6

First Edition
10 9 8 7 6 5 4 3 2 1

To Coach Virgil Jackson, for his profound influence
on Bob Mathias and for not knowing the meaning
of the word "can't"

CONTENTS

Sections of photographs appear after pages 24, 48, 66, and 90.

ACKNOWLEDGMENTS

ACKNOWLEDGMENTS TO:

Gwen Mathias, for intuition
Bill Scott, for vision
Lillian Mathias, for supporting research
Shirley Tassin, for patience and encouragement
The Tulare *Advance-Register,* for its Mathias chronicles
The late Maxwell Stiles, a "dynamite" source

FOREWORD

As one who spent several years training for an Olympic decathlon effort in 1976, I have never ceased to marvel at the Tulare, California, teenager who came from obscurity to take top honors in 1948.

To have won the gold once was not enough for "Mighty Mathias"; he went on to repeat his feat in 1952. What's more, I am of the opinion that he would have achieved victory again in 1956 had he dedicated his life to that end as today's decathletes are prone to do. After all, Bob was a young, mature twenty-five at the time of the Melbourne Games.

While in training for the Montreal Games, I devoured every scrap of reading matter I could find about previous Olympic decathlon winners, knowing that I could learn from each of these trailblazers. I eagerly read what articles I could find about "Modest Mathias," and I only wish I could have had a copy of this interesting, informative, entertaining book about my good friend, the "grand old man" of Olympic decathletes.

Bob Mathias: The Life of the Olympic Champion is a warm, inspiring book. But then, Bob Mathias is a warm, inspiring man.

BRUCE JENNER

INTRODUCTION

Thorpe, Osborne, Bausch, Morris, Mathias, Mathias, Campbell, Johnson, Toomey, Jenner. In the fifteen Summer Olympics held since the decathlon was instituted, Americans have won the ten-event competition nine times. Only one man has won twice—the first time at age seventeen. Some say Bob Mathias is the greatest athlete of all time. Few would deny that the claim has some merit.

A gold medal in the decathlon is the pinnacle of athletic achievement, the result of natural talent, a rare strength, fine-tuned conditioning and timing, and unusual restorative powers. Someone once said that winning the event requires a will of iron, a desire of bronze, the diversity of silver, and the endurance of gold. Amen.

To win the competition once is considered extraordinary; twice, incredible; at age seventeen, almost superhuman.

How does a person so young handle the applause after so great a feat? Lesser men would have succumbed to the lures of "superstar" status—not Bob Mathias. He has continued to be the solid citizen, holding fast to the values and ideals of his small-town upbringing in Tulare, California.

Quietly, he has given generously of his time and effort to innumerable civic, charitable and athletic causes. For eight years he served his country and the State of California as U.S. Congressman. Now he has returned to the Olympic movement —where he belongs—as Director of the U.S. Olympic Training Center at Colorado Springs.

A popular contemporary notion laments the fact that we have few real heroes around nowadays. Bob Mathias must surely be counted in that number, however small it might be. (Of course, anyone under thirty years of age was born after Bob's second triumph in 1952.) If you know Bob, you will agree he is an exceptional human being—a hero's hero. If you haven't had the pleasure, this book will help you learn more about this athlete for all seasons, model for all reasons.

BOB MATHIAS

The Life of the Olympic Champion

1

Ascent

The date is November 17, 1930.

Looking at "all the news that's fit to print," today's *New York Times* finds President Hoover "in full vigor," despite the country being in the throes of the Great Depression.

Opting for a film contract, Bobby Jones announces his retirement from golf, and Amateur Athletic Union President Avery Brundage "traces the decline of track interest to other sports" such as golf, tennis, and swimming.

And on November 17, 1930, *The New York Times*— and every other paper for that matter—takes no notice of the fact that Mrs. Charles Mathias of Tulare, California, has delivered a nine-and-one-half-pound boy.

Patience, Mr. Brundage, patience.

It is November 17, 1941. Armies sweep through Europe. In twenty days, the Japanese will bomb Pearl Harbor, and the U.S. Congress will declare war.

Stanford University, with a 6-2 win/loss record, is hoping to beat Oregon State to the Rose Bowl.

In Tulare the Charles Mathias family has a sick son to take

care of. Owing to a case of acute anemia, eleven-year-old Bob is enduring a strict regimen prescribed by his physician-father: lots of rest, countless iron and liver pills, and loads of food. In the latter case, Bob is cooperating as an obedient son should.

Patience, Stanford, patience.

November 17, 1947. This day's *New York Times* has a story about "the first section of the Friendship Food Train [pulling] into Jersey City . . . with thirty carloads of gifts from the American people to relieve hunger in France and Italy."

On the commodities market, food prices have just about doubled in the six years since 1941, and for the Mathias family, the rise in food prices is a serious budgetary matter.

Bob, seventeen years old today, is over his bout with anemia, but between football, basketball, and track a ravenous appetite is clearly in evidence. Actually, he eats just about every time his hands are free.

His Tulare track coach, Virgil Jackson, is trying to coax him into participating in additional events besides the discus, hurdles, and the high jump.

Patience, Coach, patience.

Two hundred and thirty-two days later, the front page of the August 7, 1948, *New York Times* carries this two-column headline: U.S. BOY, 17, WINS DECATHLON IN EERIE SETTING AT OLYMPICS. Below this, it says: MATHIAS BEATS ATHLETES OF 19 NATIONS IN 10 EVENTS ENDING UNDER LIGHTS.

> LONDON, August 6—Well on toward midnight in floodlighted Wembley Stadium and with only a handful of the original 70,000 spectators remaining, Robert Mathias, 17-year-old recent high school graduate from Tulare, California, won the Olympic decathlon championship. His

victory in the grueling ten-event test provided the United States with its ninth gold medal in men's track and field.

As the wearied decathlon gladiators completed under floodlights their two days of exhausting effort, Mathias, unheard of except locally until a few weeks before he gained his place on the team, scored one of the great victories of the Olympics in competition with the best all-around athletes of nineteen countries.

Wearing a sport coat and Bogart-styled "baggies" with cuffs, Robert Bruce Mathias stands on the highest of three platforms, which is decorated with the five Olympic circles. An official of the games hands the victor a small leather box containing a gold medal. Holding the award, the self-conscious teenager shifts nervously. He is the youngest person ever to win the decathlon.

Below him, on his right, is silver medal-winner Ignace Heinrich from France; U.S. teammate Floyd Simmons, winner of the bronze, is on his left.

Mathias remembers: "The official commanded us to turn to our left. Then we were facing the flagstaff, and I could see Old Glory running up to the top. The bands struck up the 'Star Spangled Banner,' and thousands of my countrymen exploded with a sound that shook the stadium. Believe me, if anyone has the words to describe what I felt at that moment, it isn't me. It was a moment for poets."

In the stands, Lillian Mathias, surrounded by other members of her family, tries without success to quiet her sobs of joy; her Robert came into this stadium a boy of seventeen. He will leave today every foot a grown man; in the eyes of some, a superman.

Dr. Charles Mathias is more pragmatic. He reflects on his

son's remarkable success and concludes that his diagnosis and treatment of Bob's anemia must have been right.

In the spring of that year, Bob had only casually heard of the decathlon, so no one was more surprised with his rapid rise as a decathlete than he. Surely, his success had to be the result of a rare combination of factors—a body made strong through adversity; a loving family; and the pairing of an easy-going, almost too relaxed personality with a remarkable capacity to concentrate intensely on the job at hand.

Some might say that Bob personified the "All-American Boy." Labels aside, however, Bob Mathias seemed simply to have had the good fortune to be equipped and prepared when opportunity arose. Just four months prior to the 1948 Olympics, Bob had never pole vaulted, had never held a javelin, had never run the 1500 meters in competition, and had seldom broad jumped or run the sprints. Discus, high hurdles, and the high jump had been his events. Now, an Olympic champion, he was at the zenith of achievement in all-around track and field; the best in the world in the two-day test.

Bob would soon become a friend of presidents and an acquaintance of world leaders. He would visit over forty countries as an American ambassador of goodwill, yet he would not lose sight of his small-town values, feeling as much at ease with a group of elementary school children as with heads of state.

He had learned from his family and early life in Tulare the need for understanding and compassion for people of all races, religions, and walks of life, and this knowledge would sustain him well as he faced the demands his fame imposed on him in the years to come.

2

The Formative Years

Robert Bruce Mathias was born into a world of economic hardship, beginning life just a year after the disastrous Wall Street crash, but he was blessed with a family headed by a hard-working, secure small-town physician. While the soup and unemployment lines lengthened in the industrial Midwest and Northeast, effects of the depression were less severe in the farming communities of the American Far West, at least for those in California's San Joaquin Valley. A medical doctor with a rural practice might not always get paid with currency, but his table was usually supplied with fresh eggs, milk, cream, butter, a cornucopia of fresh fruit and vegetables, and a variety of meats from neighboring farms, gardens, and orchards.

Eugene, the eldest son, was three years old when he acquired a brother. It was on the cold, damp morning of November 17, 1930, that Dr. Frank Kohn, a friend and associate of Dr. Mathias, delivered the second son, who weighed a substantial nine-and-a-half pounds.

When Charles Mathias hugged his wife, Lillian, and congratulated her on another boy, she said softly, "Oh, Charles, I so wanted a girl."

The boy would make it up to her a hundred times over.

Thanks to a healthy diet, a stable homelife, and a small town full of friends, Bob grew up well-adjusted and happy, typical in just about every respect except one: as his father soon observed, his natural coordination was nothing short of exceptional. Seldom did Robert fall or stumble into things. He walked, ran, and played with an uncannily well-developed sense of balance.

Dr. Charles Mathias could recognize athletic potential, having himself been a football and track star in high school, and earning All-Missouri Valley Conference honors as left end on the University of Oklahoma team. In 1927, before he received his medical degree, he had fallen in love with and married Lillian Harris, the daughter of a merchant operating a grocery and bakery near the Indian village of Gray Horse, a large settlement in the Osage Territory of Oklahoma.

After graduation from medical school, Dr. Mathias served as intern at the San Diego Naval Hospital, then was in residency briefly at the Tulare Hospital. For the young physician, Tulare seemed to be the right kind of town: neither too small, nor too large, it was friendly and clean—a nearly ideal place to raise a family. It was love at first sight. Following a hitch with the Veterans Bureau, Dr. Mathias took his bride back to Tulare. It was to be a good choice.

The doctor's adoption of the small San Joaquin Valley town would prove to be a wise move beyond his fondest expectations. As his children grew to playing age, they were enveloped by a caring, carefree lifestyle where everybody knew everybody. An extended family in Tulare included relatives, neighbors, the druggist downtown, and especially the parents of one's friends. And for the Mathias children, there were many pals.

For little Robert, there were four boys in particular that were almost as close as his siblings. Bob Abercrombie, lived a block down the street. Bob Hoegh, who would later attend

Kiski Prep School with Mathias, was only eight blocks away. Rounding out the quintet were Sim Iness and Dane Sturgeon. The clique would be inseparable as friends, teammates, and classmates through eleven years of elementary, junior, and senior high school.

Two of the five would become internationally famous.

In those years, happiness was not something ordinary people tried to buy. Bob says he can't remember ever getting an allowance. "Actually, I didn't need anything. I had friends; I had family; I had fun. Why would I need an allowance?"

Because he stuck close to his older brother, Eugene, Bob had a second set of friends, which meant that he often played with children a couple of years older than himself. He was able to keep up with the best of them in climbing, running, throwing, wrestling—doing well enough in these activites to be accepted into their group. As if in repayment for the generous attention Gene paid him, Bob found time for his little brother, Jimmy, who was three years his junior. (Starting with Eugene, each of the four Mathias children, including the youngest, Patricia, was born three years after the last, so the sibling rivalry was not as intense as it might have been.)

The backyard at the Mathias' home on East King Street had a hurdle, shot and discus pit, parallel bars, and high jump rig; it became the neighborhood playground. When the gang needed more space for organized sports, the grammar school, junior high, and high school grounds all were less than ten minutes away.

Robert did many of the mischievous things an active, small-town boy would be expected to do. From expressing early interior decorating aspirations with red paint and brush in the family kitchen, to high jumping in the next-door neighbor's flowerbed, Bob wreaked his full share of havoc. The neighbor in question would apologize, years later, for "chasing a future world champion" out of her garden.

Another neighbor, Mrs. Colin Schureman, swore that Bob learned to throw the discus by tossing her garbage-can lid down the alley. When Bob won his gold medal in London, all was forgiven. Mrs. Schureman sent him a cable which read simply, "Yippee!"

Dr. Mathias recalls the time that Bob's teacher, Margie Shannon, refused to believe her pupil when he told her the Mathias family had a new baby. (Lillian Mathias had been to a PTA meeting the week before and Miss Shannon had noted no evidence of an impending blessed event.) Bob decided to back up his claim. Unbeknownst to his parents, he took his recently adopted sister, Patricia, out of her crib, put her on a pillow in his little red wagon, and took her to school for "show and tell."

Mrs. Mathias recalled afterward, "Dad and I were about to call the FBI. We thought Patricia had been kidnapped until a neighbor, Mrs. McCourt, told us she had seen Robert heading toward school with his wagon, and there appeared to be a baby in it." So they rushed off to Wilson Grammar and arrived just as the dawdling wagonmaster and his passenger were arriving.

Lillian remembers another time when Bob was entertaining Patricia on one of the swings in the backyard. "She was about three; Bob was around nine. Instead of having her in her small swing, Robert had put her in the twelve-foot-high one we had rigged up for the boys. She apparently fell out—just let go—and went sailing through the air. Bob came to the back door and told me, 'I think I just killed Patricia.' I rushed out and found her sprawled on the ground, stunned." But, happily, uninjured.

Bob, Eugene, and Jimmy built treehouses, roller-skated the skin off their knees, rode the chains off their bikes, dug caves to use as secret hideaways, and went hunting and fishing with their father. The YMCA summer camp at Tulequoia, an hour's drive from Tulare, also had a profound influence on Bob's love for the outdoors. Swimming, in particular, was one of his favorite activities. (He remains an avid trout fisherman today.)

Lillian Mathias recalls: "When Robert was about twelve years old, he came home from a camping trip anxious to show me how well he could flip pancakes. I heard him in the kitchen at about six-thirty the next morning; he had mixed the same amount of batter they cooked at camp to serve twelve boys. Robert had a big hotcake ready to flip and, when he did, it came down on my bare foot. I'll never forget the feeling of that warm pancake between my toes."

A postcard from camp showed Bob to be a clear and direct letter writer:

> Dear Mom, Send me some shoe strings and some candy and let [brother] Jimmie send me some funny books. Robert

An ardent collector, Bob treasured bottle caps, match covers, marbles, and books. Thanks to his father's practice, he grew to have a penchant for more bizarre items: preserved tonsils, kidney stones, and an appendix.

Collecting bird eggs was Eugene's hobby for a while, and he liked to recruit Bob as an assistant. Bob served well, shinnying up tree trunks to retrieve the multi-colored treasures, until the day he put two eggs into his mouth to free his hands for a difficult descent. He hit the ground hard enough to make him bite into the eggshells, and before he knew it, two wet chirpers were squirming around in his mouth demanding daylight. Eugene promptly lost his assistant; and, it was, coincidentally, not too long after this incident that Bob tossed a cherry bomb in the upstairs bathroom while Gene was on the "throne."

Bob's mother was not a hard taskmaster, but she believed that recognizing and accepting responsibility was something to be learned early. When she stood on the front steps and blew her whistle each evening before dinner, her children knew they had better make tracks back home. They also knew that toys and sporting equipment were to be returned to their respective places. Pronto.

"Discipline was not a negative thing in our home," Bob says. "The manner in which it was applied by Mom and Dad made it easy to accept."

Chores were likewise accepted—at least, most were. "As a boy, I never could learn to enjoy washing dishes," Bob says now. "I didn't mind drying, so it wasn't a macho matter. I guess I had an aversion to getting my hands into that greasy, grimy water. I cut my share of lawns; did the roughest ranch work, including shoveling manure, and worked long days as a fruit picker; but dishwashing was still at the bottom of my list." Of course, the chore rotated among the four children, so Bob ended up doing his share.

This dislike of dishwashing brought on the famous dish towel caper. "While Dad and I were in the living room," Lillian recalls, "Robert and Gene were at the kitchen sink having a good-natured fight. When the dishes were done, though, I had to mop the floor and take down the wet kitchen curtains; both of the boys were drenched to the skin. Gene had flipped Bob with his dish rag, and vice-versa. I finally began crying and begged Dad to let me do the dishes. I suggested we put the boys to work mowing grass and raking leaves." Bob recalls the alter-cation more as "planned spontaneity" by two scheming dish-washers than mere coincidence.

In school work, Robert was coming along decently but was no great shakes as a scholar unless someone challenged him. In spelling, he was particularly weak. Why? "Because I didn't study, and it is almost impossible to learn to spell without studying.

"One day, I was fiddling and fidgeting in the back of the classroom when Miss Lois Thompson called on me to spell a simple word. I stammered, scratched my head, and gazed at the ceiling as if pondering the question would somehow magically produce the answer.

"Giving up after a few abortive attempts, I was instructed to stay after class, whereupon Miss 'T' proceeded to bawl me out. Lecturing as if *she* had been let down, she told me I could be the best speller in the class if only I spent a little time at it. She really let me have it. To be sure, she was acting, but I believed she was as incensed as she looked.

"I left that class so angry at her that I swore I'd show her up. From that point on, I was always prepared, and she was right: I did become a good speller. But it was years later before I realized that Miss Thompson, God bless her, had tricked me into applying myself. I often think of her brilliant performance during the Academy Awards season."

Before the onslaught of severe anemia at age eleven, Robert Bruce was on his way to becoming quite an athlete. He was the best in his class at the shot put, had high jumped 5 feet, and was broad jumping 15 feet. "These large feet sure came in handy when I wanted to run, jump, or throw," Bob now remarks.

Later, a curious compliment would be paid his unusually large pair of feet. In the speculation surrounding him following his 1948 victory in London, one of his coaches intimated a belief that the secret to Bob's success were his "perfect feet." An unexpected comment, but not farfetched if analyzed carefully. On a take-off for the high jump, for example, the extended foot gave him several inches advantage. The same was true in running or throwing.

In addition to his athletic pursuits, Bob's interest in medicine was increasing as he accompanied his father on his rounds of house calls. Bob became such an ardent assistant, in fact, that by the time he was in junior high, he was quite adept at helping with bandages and casts, according to Dr. Mathias. His on-the-job training captured his interest so completely that he quickly learned the name of every bone in the human body. Soon, however, he would be the patient, rather than the amateur paramedic.

Anemia struck suddenly. "I remember feeling so tired I could hardly stand." The anemic condition followed bouts with chicken pox, measles, and whooping cough, all three occurring in rapid succession.

Dr. Mathias diagnosed the problem and prescribed rest, relaxation, food, vitamins, and liver and iron capsules. In the process of recuperation, however, it was Lillian Mathias who would unwittingly give Bob one of his most important allies in the rise to stardom—the ability to relax completely.

During the first few weeks of afternoon bed rest imposed by his father, Bob naturally resented the quiet times while his friends were out on the baseball field or in the backyard wrestling. Mom taught her son to lie still and think of individual parts of his body, relaxing each one through concentration. First toes, then feet, ankles, legs, all the way to the scalp. "By the time I reached my arms, I was usually asleep." (Six years later in London, between rounds of the shot put, javelin, discus, broad jump, and high jump, Bob would crawl under a blanket and relive the process—toes, feet, legs . . . Often, someone had to rouse him when his turn came, but he would pop up loose and ready, while his competitors were taut bundles of nerves.)

At other times, Bob remembers, "When I couldn't sleep, Mom read every one of Will James's Western stories to me. Often, a gaggle of my friends were in bed with me, hanging on every word."

When Lillian tired of reading, Robert and friends listened to serials on the radio. There was "Boston Blackie," "Suspense," and numerous Westerns, but his all-time favorite was "Jack Armstrong, the All-American Boy." "I used to dream that he was what I wanted to be like when I grew up," Bob says, adding that he never suspected back then that he would come close to realizing his fantasy.

In spite of his illness, he continued at a careful pace in sports. He had high jumped 5 feet 2 inches in the eighth grade, but now he played football on the reserve team and hardly participated. "I was on the B or C team," he says, "so you can imagine how much I played." When his condition worsened, his father ordered twelve hours of sleep each night. Obviously, between afternoon naps and night sleep, he was in bed a great deal of the time.

When his strength returned, it came back in spades. The gallons of milk, assorted pills, and recuperative rest contributed to a spectacular recovery. "Pretty soon mothers began calling to ask what I was feeding the boy," Mrs. Mathias remembers. "Bob liked lots of lean meat, and almost any vegetable cooked simply, without sauces and creams. He ate no chili or other hot, spicy foods nor did he drink coffee."

Later, before a competition, she would serve him half a pound of broiled steak, half a cup of fresh-frozen peas, and a cup of hot tea with lots of sugar. Bob maintains, "The sugar provided energy; the tea, stimulation; the meat kept me from starving to death before the events were over." He failed to mention the peas.

Bob was fourteen now, and he was growing rapidly. He admired Eugene, who likewise had overcome a physical problem. From a football injury to the head, Eugene had experienced paralysis of his right side, but he had surmounted that and was now doing great things both as the basketball team's captain and an all-around track-and-field point-maker. Eventually he would become a member of the Stanford University golf team.

Gene's success, after overcoming his physical hardship, fueled Bob's interest and desire. Could he become as good as his brother, he wondered.

Patience, Bob. Patience.

3

One Small Leap for Bob, a Giant Step for a Kind Man

In the fall of 1944, the mood of the country was optimistic as the Allied armies began turning the battle against the Third Reich into a spectacular rout.

In the Pacific Theater, some eighty-nine Japanese ships were sunk off the Philippines, and although VE Day would not come until May 1945, and VJ Day would not break until August of that year, the smell of total victory was in the air.

In the fall of 1944, Bob began his freshman year at Tulare High School. "Essentially I had been a lazy kid," Bob confesses. "Maybe it was a result of my long illness, or maybe it was because I was tired from growing so fast. I don't know. But basically I had been what you might call a 'non-jock.' " Although he began making his mark in sports record books later that school year, it should be noted that Robert Bruce had attracted attention somewhat earlier.

In fact, back when he was only ten years old and in the early part of his battle with anemia, the skinny, fragile-looking boy had caught the eye of Wilson Grammar School coach, W. J. "Bill" Walker. One day, as Walker was teaching Bob's brother Eugene the finer points of high jumping, Bob had unintentionally demonstrated his potential athletic prowess. Having repeatedly missed the bar at 4 feet, Eugene was taken aside by Coach Walker in an attempt to decipher why the thirteen-year-old was failing at a height he had often exceeded.

"From my vantage point at the edge of the pit," Bob remembers, "I wondered if *I* could make it. It looked attainable." So, when the coach and Gene weren't looking, he appraised the harmless-looking bar, backed up a few yards and took off. When he arrived at his take-off point, Bob let go with a lack of form that would have scared his father half to death, considering the potential for broken bones.

Form, or lack of it, notwithstanding, the grammar school high jumper sailed over the bar with inches to spare at the precise moment Eugene and Coach Walker looked up from their deliberations.

"When I got up from the sand, I could see they had discovered my transgression. Being but ten years old and concerned that I had interfered in the coach-student relationship, not to mention that I had probably embarrassed my brother, I removed the grit from my eyes, ears, mouth, and clothing and slinked away from the pit like a puppy from a newspaper."

The coach, far from being irritated, was so impressed with what he had seen that he offered, on the spot, to give Bob instruction as well.

And so the march to London and Helsinki began with one small leap for Bob, and one large step for Coach Walker. Soon he had Robert changing his form from the scissors to the roll, and in spite of considerable awkwardness the youngster was clearing 4 feet 10 inches—more than his own height at the time. (In the scissors style, the take-off foot of the jumper is the outside foot—the one farthest from the crossbar. As the jumper clears the bar, the torso is generally vertical, and the legs move in scissored fashion. The take-off for the western roll technique is executed from the inside foot, while the body, in horizontal

position, rolls over the crossbar with the downside hip above
the bar at clearance.) Bob kept making progress until, in a
junior high rally one day, he attracted widespread attention by
jumping 5 feet 6 inches. At the same tournament, the best jump
in the concurrent high school competition had been 5 feet 5
inches.

As a high school freshman, Mathias set a number of new
county records; putting the shot 49 feet 4⅞ inches, floating the
discus over 100 feet, continuing to high jump around 5 ½ feet,
and broad jumping 17 feet 8 inches.

Young Bob Mathias' whiskers were sparse, but his frame
and limbs were growing like a spring weed. Between his freshman and sophomore years, pallor gave way to robust health;
during that period he grew six inches taller and forty pounds
heavier. Much to his disappointment, he was too heavy to meet
the California Interscholastic Federation weight limit require-
ments for the B Class and was too young to play Class A.
Consequently, he was disqualified entirely from playing sophomore football.

Lillian Mathias recalls that "Robert was drinking over *a
gallon* of milk a day, eating half a loaf of bread, and meat by
the pound, plus vegetables and fruit of every kind available—
except tomatoes. He never did learn to like tomatoes." With
Eugene and Robert in mid-adolescence, and with Jimmy approaching his teens, the Mathias food budget was beginning to
feel the pinch.

During the 1945–46 basketball season, Bob helped Tulare
High earn a tie for the league championship as a second-string
center. Then, with the start of the 1946 track season, there
began a friendly competition between Bob and a teammate,
6-foot 3-inch, 200-pound Sim Iness, that would last throughout
high school. The discus was the primary bone of contention,
and with the two locked into cordial combat, Tulareans joked

that the flying saucer craze of that time was really a result of the Mathias-Iness rivalry.

After six months of basketball and track, Bob went to work that summer as a "weightlifter," loading hundred-pound bags of insecticide aboard crop dusting planes. "That was one of the few times I felt dishwashing might not be all that intolerable," he remembers. However, the combination of heavy physical exertion with ample food and sound sleep, in alliance with the natural inclination to growth, were all working well in concert. A promising year of athletic achievement was ahead for the soon-to-be junior.

When asked about his social life at the time, Mathias concedes that he had virtually none. "In the summer, I was too tired making fifty cents an hour loading crop dusting planes to think about girls. After school days when soda jerks were busy with 'skirts,' I was occupied either on a basketball court or football field or in the track stadium."

Hayrides, wiener roasts, and picnics were all popular "boy-meet-girl" occasions, but Bob's time was being tapped for sports, and he was responding willingly.

"I understand many of my classmates would pair off on the school buses taking our student body to competitions, and I've been told that it was not unusual for a few of them to be seen necking in the back seats. Meanwhile I was always on the team bus sitting next to a sweaty teammate with the two of us talking more about our competitors than about girls."

As the 1947 football season opened, Virgil Jackson, Tulare's coach, assigned the muscular "bag man" to play at a thankless position—right halfback in the modified double-wing system. Bob's duties were singular—to clear a path for the runner—and clearly he did his job well. Actually, he did it too well; he was consistently outrunning his runners. Playing on defense as well, Bob demonstrated his open-field return ability after his oversized hands snagged interceptions. So it wasn't long before Coach Jackson was letting him carry the ball. His running antics became no less awesome than his fearless blocking, or his pin-point option passing from the halfback position. Tulare's Redskins won all but one of their games that year. Jackson reminisces, "In one game, Mathias' combined running and passing yardage exceeded the total of the rest of the team."

Bob's brother Jimmy recalls a time when, in a game with East Bakersfield High, Bob nailed the opponent's best halfback a dozen or so yards behind the line of scrimmage, unintentionally breaking the boy's wrist and rendering him unconscious. "I was team mascot and water boy. Dad was team physician. After administering fumes from ammonia capsules and taping his wrist, we finally brought him to his senses with the application of a cold, soggy towel. Coming to, he looked up at Dad and me and, in a shaky voice, said something like, 'You Mathias men are something. One of you knocks me out, one brings me back to my senses, and the other looks after my broken bones.' " From Tulare High to Stanford, Mathias would make his great strength and power felt while battering many an opposing player.

Jackson says, "As a high school athlete, Robert showed the determination to excel. It was a pleasure to see him respond to coaching. With patience he would repeat and practice until he had it right, while many other athletes would come back for more coaching before they had progressed enough to warrant it."

In basketball that winter, his junior year, Bob made the starting team as center. He had the height, long arms, and strong legs with an elasticity that allowed him to jump like a kangaroo. "Bob was at once a windmill and a vacuum cleaner on the backboards," Eugene recalls, "and with his unusual coordination he could dribble the length of the court as well as any agile guard, and at breakneck speed." The results: Tulare

High tied for the league title; Mathias was second in scoring with eighty-one points in eight games.

Gene says he suggested at the time that Bob give up football and track and concentrate on basketball. "I sincerely believe he would have become an All-American, but that hardly would have compared with back-to-back gold medals in the Olympic decathlon. So I'm glad he ignored my naive counsel."

With the spring of 1947, track came around again, and the friendly rivalry between the discus men intensified. In the first meet of the season, Mathias sent the wood-and-metal plate 135 feet; friend Iness, 133 feet. Mathias also continued putting the shot, picking up several first and seconds in the event. At the same time he was becoming a whiz at the hurdles.

When the team's high jumper was injured and couldn't compete, Bob was recruited for the event (no one else volunteered). That afternoon he practiced but could only make 5 feet 5 inches.

At the meet on the next day, he began by winning first places in the discus and high hurdles. Then, with one afternoon of practice, the once-little guy who had sneaked a high jump when no one was looking not only garnered a few points, as his coach had hoped, but took it all with a 5-foot 10-inch leap. With that first place, Tulare won the meet.

However, Bob was not an automaton-like athlete, programmed to win at the expense of having little or no personality. Mrs. Mathias recalls one afternoon when she rushed to school to watch Bob run the hurdles in a meet. The gun sounded, and the young "stick jumpers" streaked by the packed bleachers. To Lillian's surprise, Bob was nowhere to be seen. Injury was the first thing that came to her mind. When she asked a nearby student why Bob was not a participant, the girl assured her that Bob had not only run the race, but had won as well. Incredulous, Lillian finally discovered Robert, who had cut his hair very short and had bleached the remaining stubble. Later, he changed his hairdo to the Mohawk style.

Bob went on to set two records later that spring in the Fresno Relays: the discus at 140 feet 6 ½ inches, and the high hurdles in a remarkable 14.6 seconds.

Meanwhile, the battle of the discus kept heating up as Iness and Mathias treated second place like the plague. With the San Joaquin Valley CIF finals serving as a battleground, Iness propelled the spinning disk to a record-setting distance of 150 feet, only to be exceeded immediately by a Mathias heave of 150 feet 8 ½ inches. To say that Iness was disappointed would be an understatement; there are many in the valley who would point to that particular contest as the reason why Sim hinted he might not return to Tulare High in the fall.

Bob, however, bungled the high hurdle event during that same meet, because he couldn't buy a pair of size-twelve shoes. "My shoes looked like they had been mangled by a road grader, but I couldn't find my size in the area." One of the patched-up, taped-up brogans came off in the middle of the race, and he completed the event with one shoe off and one shoe on.

Summer, 1947: more one hundred-pound sulphur bags loaded into crop dusters, mountains of food, sleep, and maturity.

Fall, 1947: a 6-foot 1-inch, 190-pound Bob Mathias saunters into his senior year and football practice with the gait of a gazelle, the strength of a bear, and the dedication of a beaver. The pervasive attitude of the team is one of confident anticipation. Surely, this will be a great year for the Redskins. However, a problem looms; rumor is that Sim Iness is dropping out of school. Some say he has not yet been able to shake the previous season's disappointment of setting a record in the discus one minute and losing it the next. Actually, Iness' absence is more than a problem; in the minds of his teammates it assumes the proportions of a crisis. Besides the star's track contributions, he is an outstanding tackle, now standing 6 feet 5 inches tall and weighing 245 pounds.

Soon after being informed of the suspicion that Iness was suffering a morale problem, Bob announced that he would not be competing in the discus that year; he would concentrate on other events. Whatever the reason for his change of heart, Sim returned to school, and the Redskins were off and running— not to mention passing, tackling, blocking, and scoring. With Iness on the line, and team captain Mathias at tailback, they beat a path over opponents all the way to the San Joaquin playoffs, where they lost to a "big city school," Fresno's Roosevelt High, by a score of 20–13.

Though they failed to win the championship, it did not go unnoticed that with Iness' help, Robert Bruce Mathias had netted more total yards than all the opposing teams had gained against Tulare in the regular season. He averaged more than 8 yards per try and amassed a total of 1,268 yards in running and passing. Other stats show: 14 touchdowns, 6 on kick returns; 18 passes completed from his fullback position for 350 yards; 418 yards on kick returns. Playing "both ways," the multitalented gridder also kicked off, punted, and place-kicked—his massive foot proving itself a formidable weapon for the defensive unit.

The crowning tribute would come later from none other than his friend and competitor, Sim Iness, who told a reporter that he felt Bob was the best football player in the county. Bob was not fast, Sim said, but he had drive and power and took long strides. He observed that Bob's knees came up high; when he hit someone, they knew they had been hit. He said that you'd grab Bob's knees and think you had him, but he'd rip straight out of your grasp.

In basketball, Iness described Bob as one of those slow,

deliberate, aggressive centers waiting for an opportunity; when he got one he would move in and make it count. He was a fair shot, Sim said, making most of his goals under the basket, many of them on tip-ins.

Sim acknowledged that early in high school, Bob was better at the discus than he was—at least by a few inches. But when Mathias began concentrating on additional events like the shot put and the hurdles, Iness began to outthrow him. Still, Iness predicted Bob's best event in college would be "the platter" (the discus). Sim would be proved right.

(The following season, with Iness and Mathias gone, Tulare High would not win a single football game. While fans would not be able to use the usual "wait til next year" alibi, they could at least lean steadfastly on "remember *last* year." Coach Virgil Jackson would almost lose his job after the dismal season. Undaunted, and still feeling that Bob Mathias was the best thing that had ever happened to him, he would name his son Glen Mathias Jackson in tribute to the young man who had brought him fame and fulfillment.)

Toward the end of that memorable football year of 1947, Dean Cromwell of the University of Southern California—who would be the track and field coach of the winning U.S. Olympic effort in 1948—came to town to make a speech. Some Valley residents thought the address was a ploy to attract Bob's attention in hopes of having him work to become a decathlete on the 1948 team.

Coach Jackson had believed for some time that his pupil had the body, mind, and character necessary to achieve that potential. In a column in Tulare's *Advance Register,* sports reporter Bob Crawford surmised that Jackson had visions of "making the husky youngster into a decathlon man and entering him in tryouts for the 1948 Olympic team." When Jackson heard people around town talking about it, he added credence to the speculation, especially now that a major college coach was agreeing with his own assessment of the young man's abilities.

Coach Cromwell had told the Tulare luncheon group he was addressing that they had a boy who could compete in an Olympic decathlon, but that if he wanted to make it to London he should give up the rest of the football season, as well as basketball and other extra-curricular activities, to put all of his effort into track and field.

Bob didn't take well to his suggestion. Despite being as busy as the proverbial one-armed paperhanger, he was having the time of his life. A born leader, he was captain of his football team, class president, treasurer of the Lettermen's Society, and secretary-treasurer of the YMCA Club. What's more, his social life—at least on weekends—was improving.

"Toward the end of high school, Sim Iness got a car, and our fivesome enjoyed it tremendously," Bob remembers today. "But you could drive up and down the streets of Tulare only so many times, and then it would get boring. There was nothing in the way of a hangout for teenagers. So, on occasion, we would travel to neighboring Visalia to a dance hall that had live music. We really thought we were something. However, while we jitterbugged and fox-trotted with every girl in the place, we didn't really get to know any of them well.

"I was having too much fun with football and basketball to become a one-sport athlete. Besides, loyalty ran deep in our school; we all felt we had to contribute to as many sports and activities as we could."

School Superintendant Donovan Cartwright said Bob always knew how to handle his prominent position in the school. He praised Bob's clean habits in living and in competition, adding that Bob's name meant more to his nine-year-old son, Wilbur, than Santa Claus'. Giving most of the credit to Mrs. Mathias, Cartwright said she had done the kind of job with Bob that more parents needed to do with their children.

Cartwright added that while Bob was always a good boy, he occasionally liked to get into mischief. It seemed that Robert Bruce enjoyed "experimenting" with his chemistry teacher's patience; he and his small coterie, on more than one occasion, were suspected of planting stink bombs in the laboratory. The chemistry teacher, Cartwright recalled, was a very pious man. He said he would never forget the teacher's shock when Bob and his fellow pranksters—not entirely by accident—made a great fanfare of finding a whiskey bottle (filled with water) in the innocent instructor's desk.

After the football playoffs, Mathias donned a basketball uniform and picked up where he had left off, averaging 18 points a game, ("without hogging shots," as Eugene puts it), and earning All-San Joaquin Valley honors at center.

Track season arrived, and veterans Mathias and Iness led Tulare High to victory in every one of the dual meets. Bob won all of the hurdles events. At the Fresno Relays, Iness and Mathias finished one-two in the discus. Bob set a new meet record by putting the shot 54 feet, won the high hurdles in 14.6 seconds, and took a second in the high jump. In his high school career, Robert Bruce Mathias had earned forty first-place medals and had set twenty-one records. It was no surprise when Tulare won the high school division with a total of 27 points.

That was when Coach Jackson made his move. He pleaded with Bob to think seriously about the decathlon. The seventeen-year-old had heard just enough about the ten-event competition to know that it was terribly demanding and extremely complicated. "The method of scoring, utilizing the unfamiliar metric system, scared me about as much as the challenge of ten events," Bob reflects. Coach Jackson, however, continued pressing hard for his star to give it serious consideration. Perhaps by starting in 1948, he might become a serious contender for the 1952 Olympics . . .

You were being too patient, Coach.

Two-year-old Robert Bruce Mathias.

Howdy pardner—at four.

A thoughtful fourteen-year-old freshman.

The Mathias children. Left to right: Jimmie, 6; Eugene, 12; Patricia, 3; and Robert, 9.

On his tenth birthday, Bob tries on his brand-new football gear.

Bob with his high school coach, Virgil Jackson. They are holding the trophies Tulare, and Bob, have won in a track meet during Bob's senior year.

Practicing with teammates Dick Bramer (left) and Paul Hailey (center) during his sophomore year at Tulare High School. (*Gainsborough Studio*)

Bob puts the shot at the National AAU Championships at Bloomfield, New Jersey, in 1948.

4

The Last
One Hundred Days

May 1948—one hundred days before the London Olympic
Games.

The new state of Israel is proclaimed and is immediately
recognized by President Truman. Banks are complaining about
the Treasury's refusal to advance the basic interest pattern,
holding rates at one and a half percent. Wall Street, however,
is enjoying the wildest bull market since the onset of the Great
Depression. Wonder horse Citation adds victory in the Preak-
ness to his Kentucky Derby win.

In Tulare, another young "horse" is being groomed by his
"trainer" for the Fresno Relays—and much more, if the coach
can convince Robert Bruce Mathias to go for the brass ring.

It was at the Fresno Relays that Bob became initiated,
first-hand, into the intricate competition known as the decathlon. Always willing to admit his lack of knowledge about the
all-around test, Virgil Jackson, football mentor first and track
coach second, directed his star to a group of young men who
knew all about it. Reluctantly, Bob acceded to his teacher's

wishes and approached three of the collegiate decathletes in attendance at the Fresno meet.

He talked sheepishly to Jerry Shipkey, Gay Bryan, and Al Lawrence, a trio which undoubtedly had been impressed with Bob's achievements and record-setting at Fresno, if not prior to the meet. When they learned, however, that the upstart was seeking information about the decathlon, they exchanged looks among themselves that gave the high schooler the feeling that he might have overstepped his bounds.

Mathias emphasizes that it was their description of the point system of scoring that dissuaded him even more than the arduous competition. "You are not necessarily competing against the other participants. Rather, you strive against a standard, which at the time of the 1948 Olympics was either the 1934 world record or the Olympic record, whichever happened to be best.

"For each event in which you reach or exceed the best of the two records, you receive one thousand points. Anything below the record is scaled down from one thousand points, depending upon how close or how far from the standard you are. I found it particularly difficult to adjust to the fact that you may even elect to leave an event before you have reached your maximum potential in order to save energy for the next."

Bob also learned that the laborious ten-event competition must be completed in two consecutive days, ending before midnight of the second day. The first day's order of events was the one-hundred-meter dash, broad jump, sixteen-pound shot put, high jump, and the four-hundred-meter run.

"The first-day schedule is enough to make a growing boy cry," Bob laments. "However, that back-breaking itinerary is followed on the second day with the one-hundred-ten-meter high hurdles, the discus (my favorite event), pole vault, javelin, and the fifteen-hundred-meter killer. From the several events I had heretofore tackled, I could tell at a glance that the order is geared to try you to the hilt. For instance, the one-hundred-meter run is followed by the broad jump. Your legs are already taxed by the dash, but immediately thereafter you're called upon to run and jump, landing jarringly into a pit after being airborne for over twenty feet. While the shotput is easier on your constitution, your system tends to cool down considerably while awaiting your turns, thereby neutralizing the spring necessary for the high jump that follows. Finally, as icing on the cake, you face four hundred meters at top speed to close the first day.

"The same hurry-up-and-wait, hot-and-cold schedule gnaws at tired muscles and aching bones on the next day. Beginning with a high hurdles dash, you then rest and cool off during the discus, attempt to find your speed, energy, balance, and timing for the pole vault, stiffen up during the long waits for the javelin, and then attack the mettle-testing, heartbreaking fifteen hundred meters—'the metric mile.'

"If it had not been for Coach Jackson's faith, I would have dropped any thought of the idea, but it was difficult to tell the man no. Next thing I knew, he had talked me into entering the Southern Pacific Regional AAU Games to be held in Pasadena in a matter of days. Coach convinced me this would be an ideal introductory course, enabling me to decide if I wanted to begin the long haul of preparation to the 1952 Olympics. I promised to give it a try, but I had a couple of nagging concerns: on one hand, I had to make my grades for a June 3rd graduation; secondly, I had to do my best in my usual events at the CIF finals."

It was less than one hundred days to London, and Robert Bruce Mathias had never held a javelin. In fact, none could be found in Tulare County, because it was illegal as a high school event there. (Apparently, school officials felt the spear was too dangerous.) He had long jumped and sprinted casually and had never pole vaulted or run the four hundred or fifteen hundred meters in competition.

Besides the javelin problem, which was solved by borrowing one from Fresno State College, there were other equipment crises. The high school hurdles were too short—thirty-nine inches versus the forty-two-inch college height. Not to be sidetracked by simple problems, Jackson added the three inches by tacking slats to the tops of the barriers. Then a sixteen-pound shot had to be procured.

Bob remembers: "The new hurdle height made for real consternation. Not only was the timing different, I was afraid I would get to the Berkeley meet and jump the thirty-nine-inch hurdles three inches higher than I had to, thereby slowing me down and spoiling my chances of winning. Luckily, Coach Jackson enlisted the aid of former Chico State hurdler and Tulare High basketball coach Ernie Lambrecht, who offered countless pointers."

Lambrecht could see that Bob had good style and plenty of power, though he sometimes took the hurdles too high. To get Bob to clip them closer, he put blocks of wood on top of each hurdle; when his pupil began knocking them off, he knew he was skimming the barriers correctly. In addition, Lambrecht taught the hurdler to "race" over the sticks instead of jumping over them.

In the pole vault, Bob was only able to clear a lowly 8 feet during the first week of practice, remarking in desperation at the time that coming down wasn't nearly as hard as getting up. It was definitely the hardest event for him to learn. Coach Virgil recalls: "In San Francisco, we selected from about sixty bamboo poles and found only two suitable for a two-hundred-pound vaulter."

Jackson was convinced that, as a kid, Bob had frolicked around with the pole just enough to pick up a lot of bad vault

habits that had to be broken. It wasn't until a week before his debut at the Pasadena games that Bob actually got the proper feel of the pole, according to Jackson, "but his chest had turned raw from bumping against it."

He reached 10 feet just before he left for Edwards Field at the University of California at Berkeley, where three hundred top athletes were waiting. In addition, he had finally begun to learn how to hold the javelin.

In the CIF finals at Berkeley, he was the meet's only two-event winner, taking gold medals in the 120-yard high hurdles in his best lifetime speed of 14.5 seconds; and the 180-yard low hurdles in 19.6 seconds—fast enough to leave the second-place finisher nine yards behind in his wake.

At the awards ceremony, the announcer called Bob "America's greatest hope in the decathlon." Although Bob didn't really believe this, Coach Jackson did. Word of Mathias' amazing feats was getting around, even before his first competition as a decathlete.

The coach had recently been impressed with Bob's results in an athletic ability test given at school. The test was comprised of ten events with a possible top score of one hundred and in it Bob had scored ninety-six, dropping only two points in the 330-yard dash, one in the seventy-five-yard dash, and one in the standing broad jump. The test was seen by Jackson as a form of decathlon in itself. He had been studying a decathlon book he had procured from Finland, and based on the recent test, he felt confident Bob would not be embarrassed.

His accomplishments at the Pasadena Games were testimony to the unrelenting work he had compressed into the short interlude between Berkeley and the Southern Pacific AAU Games—this in spite of the fact that he was competing in six events for the first time: the hundred, four hundred, and fifteen hundred meters, broad jump, javelin, and pole vault. In addition, the field of competitors was anything but shabby. In fact,

it included two of the collegians who had lectured him on the trials and tribulations of "decathology" at their meeting during the Fresno Relays. Present were North Carolina star Floyd Simmons, who had recently moved West; UCLA strongman Jerry Shipkey; and Al Lawrence of the University of Southern California, who was favored by some to upset U.S. Champion "Moon" Mondschein in June at the U.S. Olympic trials.

With Lawrence sidelined by injuries on the first day, however, Bob found himself five points in front of Shipkey that evening. His performance was eye-opening: 11.3 seconds in the one hundred meters; 21 feet 4 ½ inches in the broad jump; a shot put of 43 feet (remember, this one weighed sixteen pounds); a high jump of 5 feet 10 inches; and 52.1 seconds in the four hundred meters.

Pole vaulting almost proved his downfall on the second day. After a second-place time of 15.7 seconds in the hurdles and a discus hurl of 140 feet, he twice missed the vault bar at 9 feet 6 inches—several inches below his previous high. With one try left, he spent his off-time while others vaulted working out his step on another runway and came back to clear the height with inches to spare. Ultimately he reached 11 feet 9 inches, considerably higher than he had ever vaulted before.

Meanwhile, between events, Bob called on his ability to relax, and curled up under a blanket and dozed.

In the javelin, he exceeded Shipkey's excellent toss of 170 feet by over 5 feet for the best throw of his young life.

The pole vault had taxed his strength to the limit, however, and he worried about the climactic fifteen hundred meters, an event he had hardly worked on at all in practice. He plodded along, nevertheless, calling on every reserve of strength and will, and finished the "metric mile" in under five minutes.

At the end of the two-day event his final score was 7,092. The winner? A surprised Robert Bruce Mathias. His score was the highest score since 1941 to be posted in the United States,

a sobering statistic for Mondschein, Lawrence, Shipkey, and Simmons.

The crowd was abuzz with one question: "Who is this guy, Bob Mathias?" The attending press was equally perplexed. In fact, a sports editor at his desk in Los Angeles asked for verification of a telephone report that a "Bob Mathias" had won the decathlon at the Pasadena Games. He had never heard of the Tularean.

It was only fitting that he enter the National AAU Decathlon Olympic Tryouts to be held in New Jersey in late June— a meet that was to serve a secondary purpose as the Olympic trials.

Off to Bloomfield, New Jersey, went Coach Jackson and the seventeen-year-old, with Bob slightly less apprehensive than he had been on his way to the Pasadena Games. The modicum of savoir faire he had picked up there was no small comfort. As testimony to their support, the citizens of Tulare had raised the funds to cover Bob's expenses and, while the gesture was profoundly touching, it actually put more pressure on the teenager who was anxious to measure up.

Members of the press showed up en masse, like so many doubting Thomases. Surely, they thought, the Pasadena Games win by the green "whiz kid" was an aberration. They no doubt figured that Lawrence's injury during the West Coast meet and other undetermined factors had contributed to the sudden ascendancy of the California teenager. One writer reminded his readers that a decathlon man must have a powerful arm, a sprinter's speed, a weight lifter's power, a gymnast's agility, a miler's sense of pace, and the training of an acrobat. He didn't realize he was describing Robert Bruce Mathias.

Another formidable field of entrants was assembled for the Olympic tryouts, including a healthy Lawrence, a hungry Simmons, and champion Mondschein, who finished the first day

with a dazzling 4,187 points. It was his best day ever and only
five points fewer than Glenn Morris had accumulated on his
way to winning the 1936 Olympics. Simmons was second, and
way back in third place was Mathias with 3,833 points. Except
for the shot put, in which Mathias and Mondschein finished
first and second respectively, Moon beat Bob in the other four
events:

Event	Mondschein	Mathias
hundred meters	11.1 seconds	11.2 seconds
long jump	23'	21' 6 ⅝"
high jump	6' 5'	6'
four hundred meters	50.9 seconds	51 seconds

What might have been a long, sleepless night for Bob was,
in fact, a rest-filled interval for the "great relaxer." Before
turning in, he evaluated his chances and felt more encouraged
than his rivals could have imagined. Of the next day's events,
two of them—the hurdles and the discus—were his favorites,
and he was improving daily in the fifteen hundred meters and
pole vault. The javelin, still a novelty, was an unknown.

On the second day, led by Lawrence's fast clip, Mathias
ran the hurdles in 15.1 seconds, good for 900 points, while
Mondschein was left at the rear of the pack. The reigning U.S.
champion could only throw the discus 125 feet, while Bob
eclipsed his effort with a throw of 140 feet, good for 800 additional points.

Before the next event, menacing thunder clouds let loose
and Foley Field was turned into a slippery brown slough. Bob
figured his large feet would serve him well in the sea of mud—
and they did. After a ninety-minute downpour, he tied Lawrence in the pole vault at 11 feet 6 inches, with Mondschein
falling behind even farther. Virgil Jackson remembers, "The
high-jump and pole-vault pits were sand, although about three

inches of sawdust was layered above the sand. The pole-vault runway was so soggy that they poured gasoline on it and ignited it to dry out the surface."

In the quagmire, Mathias managed a javelin throw of 147 feet. While it was only good enough for fifth place, Moon finished out of the first ten, and his lead was narrowed to virtually nothing. After the fifteen hundred meters, in which Bob shaved his best time by seven seconds, the scores were tallied: Mathias finished first by 123 points, Mondshein placed second with 7,101 points, and Simmons ended up ahead of Lawrence with 7,050 points. America's decathlon team would include the top three. And the fuzzy-faced kid from the San Joaquin Valley would head it.

From the teletype of the local paper, word spread quickly: Tulare's favorite son had won the Olympic trials. Mrs. Mathias chronicles the events of the evening: "Bob called from Bloomfield, wanting to know if we would pick him up at the airport, so he wouldn't have to ride the bus home. He was exhausted, he said.

"Little did he know the locals were celebrating spontaneously, and the radio news reporters had been in to interview us. Besides the family members who would greet him on his arrival, a motorcade of local folks was being organized to escort our hero for the eleven miles from Visalia Airport."

Bob would not have to ride the bus that night.

The Price of London Gold

Between the National AAU Championship win and the departure for Great Britain, the few days in Tulare were extremely hectic for Bob. Practice sessions in preparation for the Olympics took precedence, though learning a complex scoring system also required considerable time. Clothing and equipment had to be collected and, throughout Bob's comings and goings from home, he had to deal with the persistent interest of the press. In addition, the pounding at the Pasadena Games and the battering at Bloomfield had left Bob's trusty pair of track shoes in terrible condition. However, now that he was headed for the crowning event of track and field, Dr. Mathias thought the time had come for his son to have a pair of "big city" shoes.

Dr. Mathias went on a shopping mission to Los Angeles that finally took him to a major sporting goods outlet. When the doctor informed the shoe salesman there that he needed a size-thirteen track shoe, the clerk did a double take and inquired as to the boy's age. Dr. Mathias recalls that when he told the young man his son was seventeen, the salesman replied pointedly with all the sagacity of a Socrates. He advised the customer to save his money. No boy of seventeen, he said, with a foot sized thirteen, would ever be worth his salt in athletics. Dr. Mathias didn't try to explain but he did make the purchase.

With the new shoes in hand, Bob was almost ready to fly to New York for the voyage to London and the Olympics. First, though, he conferred with his minister, Edward Sweet of Tulare's First Methodist Church. The pastor asked God to give the young competitor the strength and courage to give the best possible account of himself, both to man and Maker.

According to Bob, the crossing to England was a debilitating experience. Sea sickness and Moon Mondschein took their toll on him. Moon, who bunked with the two other U.S. decathlon contenders, Floyd Simmons and Bob, spent endless hours working out, and in the process compounded the suffering of the ailing voyager. "Between nausea and noise, I seldom slept," Bob remembers.

It also seemed to Bob that his two roommates conspired to emphasize the advantages of their age and experience over the Tulare teenager. When Moon wanted to tell a "grown-up" joke to Floyd, he would suggest that Bob leave the room. Making a big show of shaving, Moon wondered out loud whether officials would admit a contestant who was not yet shaving.

"Terra firma was a welcome friend," Bob reflects, "but it was days before my rubbery sea legs convalesced. I suspected that the European contestants, many of whom would travel to London via a short twenty-eight-mile boat trip across the English Channel, would be at a distinct advantage."

As to Bob's chances, speculation, skepticism, and detraction extended beyond the ranks of the international press. Even the coach of the decathletes, Kansas State University's Ward Haylett, was dubious. He said that Bob Mathias showed great promise, but he was not ready to state that the new U.S. champion could beat Mondschein as he had at Bloomfield. He cautioned reporters to bear in mind that Moon had been bothered by a sore arm in the field events on the second day of the New Jersey trials. To this he added magnanimously that he would work hard with Bob and felt the youngster could improve his marks.

An old Royal Air Force base in the town of Uxbridge, located some ten miles from the decathlon venue—Empire Stadium in suburban Wembley—was to serve as Bob's home during his stay. Renovated by the British, Uxbridge offered all the necessary services, and Bob recalls that when anything was lacking, it was quickly supplied. "I remember a member of our team, a farmboy, who complained about having cold feet during the night. Next evening, he was all smiles when he discovered a hot water bottle under his blanket. 'Jes' like Mama would do,' he said. To him it was a marvel." Bob, however, was not as interested in the day-to-day conveniences as he was in the practice track and the training facilities. Comfort and play would come later. There was work to be done.

Having begun his decathlon training only some hundred days before, Bob utilized the brief period before "D-Day" (August 5) to hone his performances in each event, particularly the ones that were new to him—the sprints, javelin, and fifteen hundred meters. He had come a long way since the Fresno Relays, but there was no escaping the fact that here were thirty-seven of the world's top athletes from nineteen countries waiting to do battle with him. Intensive daily workouts were essential if he hoped to do well. (They were also responsible for a couple of nagging injuries: a javelin elbow and a painful, high-jump knee.)

Nevertheless, Coach Haylett, after observing Mathias at practice, declared that his student was making progress, and he predicted that Bob would accumulate 7,400 points—an outstanding score. Of course, Haylett could not have foreseen the two days of heavy rain and subsequent mud that would hinder all the decathletes.

It was misting and chilly when Robert Bruce Mathias entered Empire Stadium on the morning of August 5th to compete before the multitude of spectators. The raw, small-town Tularean was impressed by the crowd, the colorful flags, the eternal flame—all part of the Olympic pageantry, which went back to 776 B.C. The spectacle could have been overwhelming, but Bob had disciplined himself to remember that they don't give points for nervousness or anxiety.

For 1,169 years, the Grecian games had flourished as a leveler of class and a promoter of peace. Truces between warring Greek colonies were declared so that competitors could travel to Olympia for the games every four years. Thus the word "Olympiad" evolved, denoting the four-year term between games.

In A.D. 393, the games were stopped by Roman Emperor Theodosius I following the loss of Greek independence. For over 373 "Olympiads," the games were not held. Then, in 1896, the idea of an international competition of goodwill and friendship was revived. A Frenchman, Baron Pierre de Coubertin, led the effort to return the amateur athletes of the world to the field of international competition, with the hope that they would put aside their, and their countries', jealousies and political differences. There was to be no regard for wealth, religious conviction, or race.

Thus began, in 1896, the modern cycle of games, held first in Athens. Since that year, thousands of young people had stood on the fields of competition: Paris in 1900, St. Louis in 1904, London in 1908, Stockholm in 1912, Antwerp in 1920 (after a suspension of the Games during World War I), Paris again in 1924, Amsterdam in 1928, Los Angeles in 1932, and Berlin in 1936 (where Hitler raised the voice of racial prejudice to a high pitch, and where Jesse Owens' great victories triumphed dramatically over the dictator's theories), before a world war disrupted the cycle once again.

Now it was London, 1948, and these Olympics had a special significance, promising to reestablish friendship and communication among the athletes, and perhaps even the statesmen involved or attending the competition.

In the stands that dreary London day were 70,000 people —including a few friends and four Mathiases: Bob's father, his mother, and his brothers, Eugene and Jimmy. It had been an expensive, time-consuming trip for the family, crossing the United States and the Atlantic Ocean, and Bob pledged to himself to make it all worthwhile. He would try with all his might to earn a bronze medal. If he succeeded now, he would go for the gold in 1952.

The 1948 Olympic decathlon began with thirty-five contestants; two had already withdrawn, and more would fall by the wayside during the competition.

In the first event, the hundred-meter dash, Bob took his heat in 11.2 seconds, but Enrique Kistenmacher of Argentina had the best time overall, 10.9 seconds, and took the decathlon lead.

In the next event, the long jump, Bob suffered a real heartbreak. He jumped 23 feet but landed off-balance, falling back to nullify what would have been a terrific leap. After waiting in the cold rain for thirty-four other contestants to take their turn, he came back for a 21-foot 8-inch third-place effort, while Kistenmacher added to his lead with a 23-foot jump. Frenchman Ignace Heinrich took second place.

More bad fortune awaited Bob at the shot put pit. His first attempt sailed a fantastic 45 feet, but the official in charge threw down a foul flag. The smile on Bob's face turned into a scowl. He was sure he had not fouled. In fact, though, the official explained that Bob had exited the ring above the center line of the circle, this act indeed constituting a foul in Olympic competition. Despite this ruling, however, Bob went on to post respectable points in a subsequent try, taking first place with a 42-foot 9-inch put—a distance that moved him slightly closer to the leaders, Heinrich and Kistenmacher.

In the high jump, his feelings of doom returned, as dark as the clouds above the stadium. Using the Western roll that was prevalent at the time, Bob missed twice at the 5-foot 9-inch level, a height he had exceeded on many other occasions. He began to wonder if he was choking under the pressure of international competition.

Eugene, using an old discarded press pass he had picked up off the ground at a meet in California, rushed to Bob's side. It was during his brother's visit that Bob said he wasn't worried. "They don't give points for that," he added, for his own benefit as much as for his brother's.

Under his "relaxation blanket" he searched his mind and body for the cause of his failure. When the time for his third and final try came, he felt that all of his family's dreams, and all of his coaches' work, hung in the balance. If he did not make it over the crossbar, he knew he would have no chance to bring home the bronze. As he considered how to alter his form in his final jump, his mind went back to the time in Tulare when he had committed the "indiscretion" of jumping higher than Eugene, without ever having learned the right form. "The heck with form," he decided now, and made his jump with an ugly duckling straddle that must have startled officials and spectators alike. It worked. The driving bundle of legs and arms shot cleanly over the bar. Bad form, successful jump.

Once Mathias had settled down, he continued to clear the bar until he exceeded 6 feet. His best effort of 6 feet 1¼ inches was good enough for a three-way tie with teammate Simmons and Frenchman Heinrich, and considerably better than Argentinian Kistenmacher's negligible 5-foot 7-inch attempt. However, in the strange world of decathlon scoring, Heinrich took over first place, Simmons moved into second, and Mathias remained in third.

Meanwhile, the turbulent weather was delaying all events. At eight o'clock that evening, in the next event, the four hundred meters, Bob triumphed in his heat with a time of 51.7 seconds. First and second place overall went to Kistenmacher and Heinrich, after posting 50.5 and 51.5 clockings.

Wembley Stadium was cold and dank when the lights were turned off to close the first day. Despite the cold, though, Bob felt better than he had after the first couple of events. The seventeen-year-old had tallied up his score and found to his pleasure that he was firmly in third place and not that far behind the leaders, as the scoreboard showed:

FIRST PLACE, KISTENMACHER OF ARGENTINA   3,897
SECOND PLACE, HEINRICH OF FRANCE   3,880
THIRD PLACE, MATHIAS OF U.S.A.   3,848

Meeting his family, Bob briefly greeted parents and brothers and, as if to give them the encouragement and hope he himself needed, reminded them that his best events were coming up the next day. Catching the bus back to Uxbridge, he wolfed down a meal and fell into a deep slumber before he had time to think about his mom's sleep-inducing technique. It would, however, come in handy on the second day.

There was a change in the weather on August 6—it was colder and wetter. Though 10,000 fans did not return on the 6th, the rains were still braved by some 60,000 people.

In the opening event, Bob had to face the 110-meter high

hurdles with muscles as stiff as iron bars. He was in the sixth heat, and therefore didn't get to race until 11:30 A.M. In the stands, the Mathias clan worried as the turf turned from soggy to sloppy. Bob remembers: "At the warm-up before the event, Kistenmacher applied a little psychology. He swaggered on over to me and said, 'Mathematically, I have it all figured out that you can't beat me.' " Bob did not respond.

"In the ugliest race I think I ever ran [the 110-meter hurdles], I was timed at fifteen-point-seven seconds, six-tenths of a second slower than I had achieved at Bloomfield, but I was not too dismayed, considering the lousy weather." As if being given his comeuppance by a greater power, Kistenmacher hit the last hurdle and, as a result, lost his place as one of the top three contenders. Bob did not gloat; his sore knee felt terrible, and he began the race by scraping the first barrier. "I thought surely I wouldn't make each succeeding one. It was as if I was falling the full length of the race. But Lady Luck was beginning to smile." Floyd Simmons, with a 15.2-seconds time, leap-frogged into first place, Heinrich stayed in second, and Bob held onto third.

The discus was the next event, and Bob looked forward to scoring extra points in it. It was his first love, "but not when the platter [was] wet." In spite of the slippery disk, it was a thing of beauty when Mathias released it for a fabulous toss of over 145 feet. Lady Luck, however, seemed to be having second thoughts when a Moon Mondschein throw slid along the wet grass and uprooted Bob's marker. Look as they might, the officials, aided by Bob and Moon, could not find the hole where the marker spike for Bob's toss had been driven.

While they kept looking, presscard-holder Eugene Mathias bounded out of the stands and rushed over to Bob. "He wanted me to insist that they search until they found my place," Bob remembers, "but the time was going quickly, the weather was getting heavier, and I wanted to get it all done." As if to take it out on someone else, the frustrated, embarrassed officials sent word up into the audience threatening to disqualify Bob if any U.S. official came onto the field to look for the marker hole. Finally, they gave up looking and "awarded" him 144 feet 4 inches, probably less than he deserved. Bob was unable to better that mark, but he was not complaining. It was not only *his* best but *the* best of the day as well; he picked up 834 points, to 509 for Simmons, 739 for Heinrich, and 744 for Kistenmacher.

Simmons, in the lead at the time, did not deal well with the wet dish. With a disheartening 107-foot best, he dropped to fourth place in the overall scoring. Heinrich stayed in second place with 5,452 points, while the Tulare youngster moved from third to first with 5,500. Perhaps it was only his imagination, but the ponderous clouds above seemed to part momentarily. It was a good omen, and as he began to realize he was doing fairly well in the competition, he also began to feel terrifically hungry.

At noon the rain had turned to torrents. The officials, seeing it might be difficult to complete the competition before the appointed hour of midnight, persuaded Bob and the others to eat a meagre box lunch rather than break for a substantial meal.

Again in the interest of time, the pole vaulters were then divided into two groups; Bob was in the second group, which meant more waiting, the stiffening up of joints, and a generally miserable late afternoon. Bob used the delay to his advantage, though, as he took the opportunity to slip under his blanket, out of the rain, to concentrate on relaxation. It was not easy; mostly, all he could think of was steak and potatoes, medium rare roast beef, a gallon of milk, fish and chips, ham on rye (no tomatoes), topped off with strawberry scones. Still, he did manage to achieve, intermittently, a state of real relaxation.

When the first group of vaulters laid down their poles, Heinrich had moved ahead with 6,974 points; Simmons had rallied ahead of Kistenmacher with 6,950 points. Between the discuss event and the call for the second group of vaulters in late afternoon, Bob would have had time for a ten-course dinner at King George's table. It was now 7:30 P.M., and he felt hungrier than ever. In his weakened predicament, he made a risky decision not to vault until the bar was raised to 10 feet.

When he passed up his turn, Gene came bounding onto the field to convince Bob that any height was better than none—and went back just as quickly. The strategy was a big gamble, but Bob wanted to try it. "Gene worked me over pretty well, and he made good sense, but I simply had to conserve my diminishing strength."

Night fell before the 10-foot level was reached. Still Bob waited. Weak lights were turned on. A white tennis shoe was fixed opposite the take-off box as a marker, while a handkerchief was tied to the bar. Bob needed a good showing in the pole vault and javelin, because he was weak in the final event—the fifteen hundred meters.

Mathias not only cleared 10 feet handily, he achieved what he wanted: a final vault of 11 feet 5¾ inches. He went on to try 11 feet 9 inches twice, but missing, decided to stop in the interest of safety. "I could barely see the take-off point and couldn't see the bar until I was on the way up, so I decided to withdraw from further competition rather than risk a serious injury that would have snuffed out our chances completely." Now, Bob was being as defensive as he was offensive. "I decided to put my eggs in the javelin basket."

He would have to excel in throwing the spear because Heinrich needed only a fair time in the "metric mile" to exceed 7,000 points. Kistenmacher, Simmons, and Mondschein had been in the first pole vault group and, consequently, had not only completed that event, but the javelin and fifteen-hundred-meters event as well before Bob had vaulted for the first time. Before Bob even got to the javelin, all three had already left the stadium, and the field was a quagmire.

The setting at 10:15 P.M. was eerie indeed. Rain clouds hung over the stadium and dim lighting gave the officials, scurrying about with flashlights, a ghostly appearance. All but the most ardent spectators had departed for warmer, dryer surroundings. However, the javelin was Bob's present challenge, and he knew he had to meet it. The minister's words came back: "Give the best possible account of yourself." Others, Bob thought, had produced under the pangs of worse hunger and with less strength.

On his first try, he fouled. He went back to the blanket, where he contemplated the situation in a haze of weariness. "Relax, darn it, relax!" he told himself. "Remember, toes first, then the foot, ankle, calves, knees . . ." The automatic responses he had learned at eleven years of age worked when he made his next throw. His body's restored agility, fed by the momentary lapse in tension, did the trick. On his second attempt, the long, wooden wand went streaking through the night, as if propelled by an invisible jet. The little men with flashlights converged on the lance. Distance: 165 feet 1 inch. Points: 593. Bravo! The squishy sod had been conquered by Bob's size thirteen mudders, and his javelin elbow had relaxed long enough to provide the desired "catapultic" effect.

While Bob was performing so well in the javelin, Heinrich was running the fifteen hundred meters. Fatigue hit the Frenchman hard, and his *amour-propre* must have suffered deeply. Still, he finished ahead of Simmons, ending up with a total of 6,974 points.

Bob went back to the little brown score book. Coming up to the start of the metric mile, the upstart needed 194 points to win. If he finished in under 6 minutes, the world crown of track and field would be his, but that was not at all assured. Determination would have to take over where energy and strength had departed. Large feet are a blessing—when you have the muscle to move them. Their size would now be a hindrance.

Eugene had promised Bob that he would time each of his four laps and, thanks to the press pass, would be positioned so that he could let his brother know how he was doing each time around.

Lillian Mathias described the race to her friend, Maxwell Stiles, who was on assignment with *Sports World:*

> Just before the three men went across the field to the start of the fifteen hundred meters, the coaches told Bob that he could beat Heinrich by running the fifteen hundred meters in six minutes. Gene came and told me this. I didn't think Bob could do it; he looked so tired and drawn. He appeared to be utterly exhausted. He had been out there for twelve hours; and although he had a box lunch, cubes of sugar, and various forms of nutrition pills, he told me after it was over that he had never been so hungry in his life.
>
> His father, Jimmy, and I were down as close to the track as we could get. The stands were empty, the only activity being up in the press box, on the field, and among our little group of diehard fans. . . . We could see the orange spurt of the flame when the gun started the runners, but the fog was so dense we could not distinguish Robert from another runner, Peter Mullins. Both wore white satin suits. . . . Eugene was over in the infield side of the track where he could call out the time of the laps to Robert. Andersson [of Sweden] came by us first, then Robert about twenty yards behind him and Mullins about the same distance back of Robert. Robert was trying to keep up with the Swedish boy. Gene yelled to him to slow down, but he didn't do it. We didn't see them again until they came around for the end of the second lap with Robert still about the same

distance behind Andersson. Again, Gene shouted
to him to slow down; but he still didn't listen. He
figured that if he could stay close to the Swede,
he would run fifteen hundred meters well under
six minutes, but Gene was afraid he would col-
lapse and not finish at all.

The third time around, Robert had definitely
slowed down, not because he wanted to but because he had to; he was pretty far back of Andersson now. That was when I really thought I'd die.
He had one more lap to go, and I really felt that
he couldn't do it. He was so very tired. A small
bunch of boys from Pepperdine College in Los
Angeles were yelling, "Come on, Tulare," and it
gave us all heart to know we had friends over
there somewhere in the dark.

Andersson came in to finish all alone. Robert was way back in the dark, somewhere on the
other side of the track. . . . I think all of us were
praying. We could only stand there and wait for
him. We could not see him at all, didn't even
know just how far behind he was. We had seen
others fall to the track. Was that what had happened to our boy? None of us knew.

Pretty soon, here he came. He wasn't running, just jogging. His head was down, his hands
just swinging and he seemed to be watching the
track. The boys from Pepperdine began whooping it up some more to "Come on, Tulare!" I just
stood there and bawled and prayed he would
stand on his feet until he crossed the finish line.
When he had about twenty meters to go, something seemed to happen to him that snapped him
out of it. He threw his head back and speeded up,
as if he had just suddenly realized that he was
nearing the finish and not still out there alone in

the dark, miles from home. He started to run with
his arms up again. He crossed the line standing
up, and his father and one of the trainers ran out
onto the track to catch him. They walked him up
and down about ten minutes. His feet had
cramped, and he was sick to his stomach.

After the longest 5 minutes and 11 seconds Bob had ever
endured, he crossed the line with 354 points. At 10:30 P.M.,
Greenwich Mean Time, the ordeal was over. He had won. He
had overtaken Heinrich, the Frenchman. The final results:
Mathias, 7,189; Heinrich, 6,974; Simmons, 6,950; and Kistenmacher, 6,929. The boy had done a man's job.

As soon as he could reach the family, Bob leaned into the
comfort of his mother's arms. Patting her on the back, he asked,
"Are you happy, Mom?" "Oh, yes, son, and so proud," she
said. "But never again," she added, "it's too hard." Eugene and
Jimmy were wildly excited and slapping their brother's sagging
shoulders. The two had struggled vicariously along every inch
of their brother's journey to the top of the mountain. "Coach
Gene" had been helping Bob in the hurdles, high jump, and
discus ever since the days at Wilson Grammar school. As for
Dr. Mathias, try as he might he could not erase from his mind
the image of a listless, pallid eleven-year-old in bed after school.
Bob had come a long way. Heinrich's coach came over to the
celebrants to ask, "What do you feed him?"

Back in the dressing room, a reporter asked Bob what he
was going to do to celebrate. "Start shaving, I guess," Bob
replied. When asked what kept him going, Bob maintained it
was his mother. "She had been so worried about 'her boy'
competing against all those grown men. Looking back, I can see
that she was not only concerned about my physical well-being,
but also about my emotional wounds if I had failed to give a
good account of myself."

What was late evening in London was early afternoon in Tulare, where radios were tuned in for any news available. The Rotary Club meeting of that day lasted longer than usual, due to interruptions for late-breaking information. At the Elks Club, members were milling around, ready to celebrate or commiserate depending on the outcome of an event taking place some 6,000 miles away.

With five Mathiases in London, and Patricia enjoying a vacation in Kings Canyon National Park in California, Bob's grandmother, Mrs. Martha Harris, welcomed the support of neighbors and friends to help minimize the barrier of distance.

Coach Virgil Jackson was a bundle of nerves. How helpless he was—he in Tulare, his green young protégé in London fighting against mature men of resolve and experience. Mixed in with his anxiety, there must have been a sense of tremendous pride. Bob might not win, but with less than one hundred days of decathlon experience, he was making a whale of a showing.

When the bulletin finally came over the teletype machine in Tulare's *Advance-Register,* word of Bob's victory broke loose a dam of pent-up apprehension and turned the tension into a flood of rejoicing and relief. People poured out into the streets, factory whistles blew for the greater part of an hour, and fire engines drove through town with sirens screaming the good news. Horns blaring, hundreds of autos for miles around converged on the town, creating Tulare's best-remembered traffic jam. This is how Virgil described his reaction:

> I was pretty excited, after Bob had made the Olympic team, but I was fit to be tied that second day of the decathlon at London. I was in the office of one of our two newspapers, the *Tulare Bee,* receiving the news as fast as it came in over the teletype. After the pole vault, I figured he was in. When the news came through that Bob had won

At the 1948 Olympics in London. Bob is looking relaxed—before the ordeal of the decathlon begins.

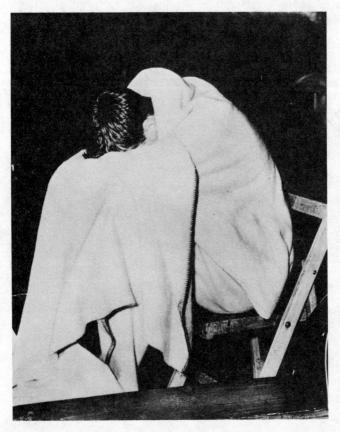

Before making his final high jump attempt, Bob uses his patented "blanket" technique to rest.

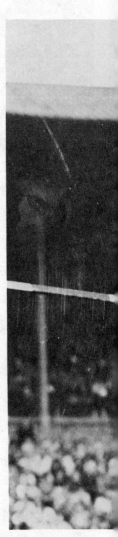

Mathias clears 6 feet 1¼ inches, his best jump ever.

The night of his winning his first gold. "Are you happy, Mom?"

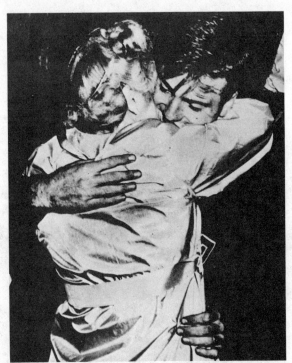

The next morning, in his room in Uxbridge, Bob is flanked by Guinn Smith, left, the winner in the pole vault, and Mel Patton, right, the 200-meter gold medalist, as he reads a newspaper account of his victory. (*Wide World Photos*)

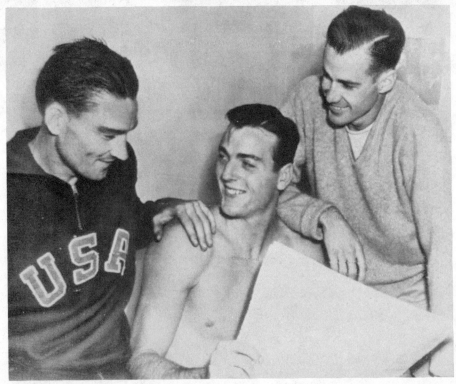

At the top at age seventeen. Ignace Heinrich, right, from France is the silver medal winner, and Floyd Simmons, left, has won the bronze.

Special edition of the Tulare *Advance Register.*

Tulare gives its local hero a welcome home. (*Prescott Sullivan*, SAN FRANCISCO EXAMINER)

A family photo after the London win. From left, Bob, Patricia, Dr. Charles Mathias, Lillian Mathias, Eugene, and Jimmie.

Bob's friends gather in his bedroom clubhouse after London. From left, Bob Hoegh, Bob Abercrombie, Sim Iness, Bob, and Dane Sturgeon. (*H. Lee Hansen Photography*)

At a banquet in Los Angeles after London, Bob has the opportunity to meet a great athlete from an earlier era, fellow Olympic decathlon champion Jim Thorpe.

At Tulare Stadium, a group of young fans surround their idol.

and everybody in town went mad, I somehow or other managed to walk out of that editorial office and down to the street. I remember the auto horns honking and the shrill sound of the sirens. I remember the faces of the people who were jumping and running all around, and I remember shaking off someone who said I looked as if I needed a drink, and he would buy me one.

I don't know how I got there, but later I found myself alone, in a city park, sitting on a park bench for twenty minutes and crying like a baby. Things like that just don't happen to a high school coach, especially one who doesn't know any more than he is supposed to know, but it had just happened to me.

Of Jackson, Olympic Coach Cromwell later told Maxwell Stiles, "Virgil Jackson, like thousands of others in America, is a much more capable coach than he has been given credit for being. It is from that source, the wonderful high school coaches throughout America, that we get these kids. In reality, the work on these college athletes you hear about all the time has been done by these high school coaches, men just like Jackson. They make the college coaches look good."

And about that legendary day, Mrs. Ester McNeil, Bob's teacher at Cherry Avenue Junior High, had this to say to the *Sports World* correspondent:

On the final day of the decathlon in London, I was taking therapeutic treatments for my arthritis at the hospital, which is on the edge of the city. The whistles and the bells were to go off all over town as a signal if Bob had won, but nurse Nancy Jean McCallister and I didn't expect to hear any of this because of the noise made by the

therapeutic machinery, so the nurse telephoned
the papers. She was told that Robert was leading,
but the final news had not come in. A few minutes
later, just as Nancy Jean was picking me up off
the bed, the bombs went off at the nearby Fair
Grounds. I shouted, "Oh, he won!" She jumped
and screamed and almost dropped me. Then we
both sat there on the edge of the hospital bed, and
the tears just streamed out of our eyes.

By this time, a national park ranger at a station nearby
had notified Patricia that her brother had won. She later said
that she and her friends dressed up and went into the nearest
town. She went into an ice cream parlor and asked if there
was a message from her brother, Bob Mathias, who had just
won the Olympic decathlon. "I knew there wouldn't be a
message," she says now, "but I wanted them to know he was
my brother."

Folks in the long line at Tulare's Western Union office,
waiting patiently to wire their congratulations to their favorite
son, were soon reading an extra edition of the *Advance-Register* with the banner headline, MATHIAS WINS DECATHLON
TITLE.

In London, by the time all of the congratulations were
acknowledged, it was past midnight and the Mathiases could
not find transportation back to their quarters. Walking part of
the way, they were finally given a lift by a reporter.

For Bob, there was no celebration that night, except for a
heart-felt tribute to the goddess of sleep. Awakened the next
morning at ten o'clock with telegrams from all over the world,
he wanted to roll over and sleep for another nine hours. Only
when he read the message from President Harry S. Truman, did
the modest young man begin to fathom the dimensions of the
feat he had accomplished. The president's telegram said:

BY WINNING THE OLYMPIC DECATHLON, YOU
HAVE DEMONSTRATED ABUNDANTLY THE
GLORY OF AMERICA IN ITS YOUTH. IN THE NAME
OF THE NATION TO WHICH YOU HAVE BROUGHT
SUCH AN OUTSTANDING DISTINCTION, I EXTEND
HEARTY CONGRATULATIONS. ALL OF YOUR FEL-
LOW AMERICANS ARE PROUD OF YOU.

For a few glorious moments on August 7, 1948, the eyes
of the world were focused on the courageous young athlete
from a small town in California. Standing between his teammate, Floyd Simmons, who placed third, and silver medalist,
Ignace Heinrich, Bob felt immensely proud and pleased beyond
words for having lived up to Reverend Sweet's entreaty to give
the best possible account of himself to God and man.

"When my own child stood out there with eighty-two
thousand people at attention," said Lillian Mathias on her return, "and they raised the flag, and the massed bands played the
'Star Spangled Banner' just for him, I thought my heart would
burst."

Bob Mathias had achieved what fewer than a dozen men
had accomplished in the modern cycle of the Olympics, but he
had done it at age seventeen. No one else had ever done it before
the age of twenty-two. As the strains of the "Star Spangled
Banner" filled Empire Stadium, his thoughts were of getting
back to high school friends, a root beer shake at the drug store,
sandlot football, and a few days of tranquility before leaving his
hometown for prep school. Tranquility would not come for a
long time, though. Even now, his new public was waiting for
him in Paris, Belfast, and Dublin.

On departure from London, Bob was asked by more than
one reporter whether he would defend his title in 1952. Bob
responded that he would not do it again for a million dollars.

Patience, Bob . . .

6

Relief Is Spelled
"K-I-S-K-I"

By September 1948, Bob Mathias and his Tulare High classmate, Bob Hoegh, were on board a two-engine airliner flying
from San Francisco to Pennsylvania to enter Kiskiminetas
Springs Preparatory School. Telling his folks goodbye at the
airport had been tough for Bob. The departure felt so final,
knowing he was probably leaving the comfort and security of
home for good.

Still exhausted from weeks of concentrated, post-Olympic
activity, Bob reclined the back of his seat a few notches and
relaxed. Hoegh was already sleeping. In a semi-conscious state
of drowsiness, the world-famous celebrity tried to understand
the changes that had taken place in his life since Easter—
changes that had taken him from a happy-go-lucky high school
senior to U.S. decathlon star to Olympic decathlon champion. It
was difficult to fathom. Some mornings, he would awaken, and
for a split second, he would think he had dreamed it all. . . .

The last time he had been aboard a plane, he had been
flying from San Francisco to Visalia Airport near Tulare with
a full contingent of reporters, their microphones turned on

and cameras clicking. Bob had, in fact, been spending a lot of his time after the Olympics en route from one place to another.

Immediately after the competition, he had left on a post-Olympic exhibition tour of France and Ireland. Then on August 27, he and 167 other U.S. Olympic athletes had returned to America to a welcome of spraying, whistling, hooting boats in New York harbor. A planned ticker-tape parade, however, was canceled by officials when the ship arrived early, and the restless athletes scattered to all points of the compass. Bob stayed in town for a day to receive a National Hi-Y award in recognition of the service he had performed for that organization. He and brother Gene also took in a Yankee-Cleveland doubleheader as guests of Red Strader of Modesto, California, who, like Bob, had been a San Joaquin Valley athletic star. Strader was coach at the time of the New York Yankees professional football team.

An overnight flight took them to San Francisco, where they were met by a press anxious to hear, first-hand, words of wisdom from the hero. Reporters were intimidating, but soon, Bob thought, he would be home in quiet, peaceful Tulare. As it turned out, Tulare was not quite as peaceful as he had expected.

Five thousand Tularaens had turned out at the airport to give him a rousing welcome. Engaged in an on-flight press conference, Bob was amazed when he saw the crowd gathered below in the one-hundred-degree heat. "It looked like the whole valley was out to greet us, and all I could think of was: I hope they're not going to ask me to make a speech." They wouldn't; not yet.

Carried above the pressing crowd on the shoulders of his Tulare High teammates, the embarrassed victor was deposited into the waiting arms of his family members, who were standing near an open convertible that would take the group to Tulare.

Through the milling, smiling mob, Bob finally clinched his dad in a bear hug, kissed Mom, slapped Jimmy on the back, and then grabbed Patricia and swung her around. He had not seen "his favorite sister" since his departure for London. Gene, having lost twenty pounds during the trip accompanying Bob, put his mother on notice that he had missed her cooking. After untangling himself from a bevy of screaming co-ed classmates, Bob and family were then directed to the blue convertible that would lead the motorcade to Tulare. To the strains of "Hail Tulare," played by the Tulare High band for their former clarinetist, Robert Bruce Mathias, the procession pulled out, with Bob sitting on the back of the rear seat; his family was seated below.

Along the eleven-mile route, Bob waved and shouted to friends and neighbors, calling most of them by their first names. Because of his popular athletic exploits in high school, everyone felt he or she knew Bob well, and he knew practically every one of them.

Before ten thousand rejoicing people at City Hall, Dr. Elmo Zumwalt, Sr., mayor of the city, welcomed the world champion: "We're all proud of you, Bob. The evidence of Tulare's feeling is in sight for everyone to see." (The mayor would someday have an internationally famous son of his own —Admiral Elmo Zumwalt, Jr., who would become Chief of U. S. Naval Operations.) The crowd roared its approval when "hizzoner" gave the decathlete the keys to the city. Telling the audience of his plans, the weary traveler said they included as much rest and relaxation as he would be able to squeeze out of his crowded itinerary.

The *Advance-Register*, recording the outpouring of veneration, called the event the biggest day in Tulare's history. There were balloons, banners and bunting, a movie marquee with a welcome message, stores closed for business but sporting

"Mathias" window displays, and factories and creameries blowing their whistles.

It was a proud Sim Iness who followed his competitor and friend back to his home to learn first-hand how it all felt. While Sim had missed making the Olympic team in the discus, he was still contemplating whether or not he would give it another whirl in 1952. Soon, friends, neighbors, and the press began leaving the Mathias home; after downing the traditional quart of milk, Bob went up to his bedroom and fell into bed.

On the following evening, a capacity crowd of eight hundred attended a formal testimonial banquet in the Tulare County Fairgrounds cafeteria. Honored guests included Governor Earl Warren, later to become U.S. Supreme Court Justice, and Glenn Morris, the decathlon champion of the 1936 Olympics. Still holding the record of 7,900 points at the time, Morris said, "When my decathlon record is broken, I hope Bob will do it." He would.

The last word that night came from Bob himself: "The biggest thrill in my life was when I stood on the victory stand in Wembley Stadium, but I will remember the parade you held for me and this banquet longer than anything in my life."

Following the tumult in Tulare, there was fervor in Fresno, where hundreds feted the champion at a gathering in Ratcliffe Stadium. Sports fans in Los Angeles, 77,000 strong, and throngs in Sacramento joined in the celebrations. Delighted, but surprised, Bob kept his speeches short.

After the hoopla of his homecoming died down, Bob began getting organized to leave for prep school. One afternoon, Mathias and Hoegh went over to the playground for a couple of hours to talk and pass the football. Before long, a crowd of admiring kids collected on the sidelines. It was this obvious impression his victory had on the town's children that pleased Bob most.

Julius Friedman, reporter for the *Advance-Register,* said later that he felt Bob's victory and his all-around sportsmanship in school had done more to combat juvenile delinquency in Tulare than any other factor. A legacy indeed. . . .

"Please fasten your seat belts, and return your seats to the up-right position," Bob heard faintly over the whir of the DC–3's engines. He had been sound asleep.

With the thumping of the wheels on the Pittsburgh runway and the revving of the propellers it was a relief for Bob to know he could shortly take his six-foot-plus frame out of the confining seat. It would be a relief, too, for Bob to leave the public spotlight for the relative serenity of Kiskiminetas.

In early 1948, before the pursuit of his decathlon fortunes, Bob had applied for admittance to Kiski, as the school was known, for several reasons. His extensive tri-sport travels took him away frequently from classroom and homework, and Bob, a C-plus/B-minus student, felt a need for supplementary scholastic work before launching his collegiate studies. He hoped to go to Stanford, where his brother, Eugene, was enrolled, and Kiski had a good record of preparing young men for Palo Alto pursuits. Gene's close friend, Bob Scott, had gone to Kiski and recommended it wholeheartedly, and Bob's lifelong friend, classmate, and teammate, Bob Hoegh, was also planning to attend.

Kiski was definitely different. Bob describes his routine as follows: "Every school day was divided into three subject segments, each following a study period. There could be no excuse for not being prepared. Sports were scheduled after each day of school work, between three-thirty and five-thirty. For those whose scholastic standing could afford the time, other extracurricular activities were offered every evening."

When Bob arrived on campus, there was a tendency

among students, coaches, and teachers to soft-pedal his achievements, which pleased him to no end. There was some natural
curiosity, but no one seemed bowled over. Kiski had prepped
its share of athletes, including Harry Stuhldreher, one of Notre
Dame's legendary Four Horsemen. Prior recognition or not,
here one had to prove oneself again.

When football season arrived, the Kiski coach, Jimmy
Marks, Jr., sought to persuade Mathias to switch his interest
from the fullback position to end or tackle, explaining that two
well-qualified veterans were returning for that backfield slot.
With courteous determination, Bob assured the coach he would
take his chances. Intimating that previous achievements at that
position didn't impress him, Marks went out of his way, it
seemed, to make things difficult for Bob. Of course, the coach
was between the proverbial rock (his returning lettermen) and
the hard place (an Olympic champion). The coach eventually
came around, however, and Bob started the season at fullback.

The coach's choice paid off in the very first game against
Indiana State Teachers College: Kiski's only touchdown was
scored by "Marauding Mathias." In the second game, Bob's
booming punts helped keep the opponents backed up and score-
less. Score: Kiski, 32; Washington and Jefferson freshmen, 0.

The worm turned in the third game, as Cornell's freshmen,
a much heavier lot, crushed Kiski 24–0. Against Western Reserve Academy, Kiski was trailing 13–10, when Mathias ran
back a late game interception to lock up a 17–13 victory. Assisting heavily in Kiski victories in the next two games, he contributed pass receptions for touchdowns against the Grove City
College freshmen (20–0), and the West Virginia Frosh (7–6).

Although fumbles led to defeat in the final game, Bob had
shown his talent in all seven of the season's contests, and the
folks at Stanford were no doubt relishing the good news about
their player-to-be. Coach Marks just couldn't say enough about

his fullback. Besides Bob's running ability, Marks praised his spirit and leadership, as well as his speed, blockbuster blocking, and kicking ability.

The coach's positive remarks were a fitting prelude to the news that Bob had been nominated by the Pacific AAU as its candidate for the prestigious James E. Sullivan Memorial Award, presented each year to the amateur athlete doing the most in the interest of sportsmanship.

The accolade brought renewed invitations for public appearances. In what must have been one of the shortest speeches on record, Bob told the Pittsburgh Quarterback Club, "It was a privilege to take part in the Olympics." That was it. Ten words. At the Banquet of Champions in Toledo, he rubbed elbows with the likes of Stan Musial, George Mikan, Joe Di-Maggio, Ben Hogan, Jack Kramer, Charlie "Choo Choo" Justice, and other established greats.

Soon afterward, he learned that Tulare had been selected as the site of the national decathlon meet for 1949. At one point he had been tempted to "hang it up"—to coast through the remainder of the term at Kiski, attend Stanford, and enjoy football—if the opportunity presented itself. But now, he decided to commit himself to defending his national title in Tulare and his Olympic title in Helsinki. It was not a matter of Tulare expecting his participation; instead, he wanted to return something to the town that had given him so much. It was a responsibility, and it would be an enjoyable one.

With the decision made, he could hardly wait to handle the discus, javelin, shot, and pole again. Just thinking about jumping, running, and hurdling started the adrenaline racing through him. In the carefree days of Kiskiminetas, he had put aside the thought of ever decathloning again—among other reasons because he didn't want the press coverage and other attention which a positive decision would attract. (Some said that it was a fear of failing the second time around.) Bob, looking forward to making the announcement to Tulareans in person, left the snows of Pennsylvania for the joys of Christmastime in the lush green San Joaquin Valley.

Los Angeles Mirror sports editor Maxwell Stiles spent Christmas of 1948 with the Mathias family and wrote about his visit when he returned to the city:

> They were all together, glowing in their pride that one of their number, eighteen-year-old Robert, had become famed as the greatest all-around athlete in the world. . . .
>
> Robert . . . divided his time today among the pleasures of sleeping, drinking quarts and quarts of milk, opening Christmas presents and being the genuine pal of the neighborhood small fry. Every kid in Tulare county between the ages of five and seventeen is out to become another Bob Mathias. They all do what he did, train as he trained, eat what he ate, don't smoke because he doesn't smoke. The kids of grammar and junior high school age are his devoted slaves. Bob is their idol and their god. . . .

Back at Kiski after the Christmas break, Bob was concerned one afternoon when the headmaster asked to see him after class. Concern gave way to shock, then to pride, when he was informed that he had won the James E. Sullivan Memorial Award. Of the 252 ballots cast by U.S. sports leaders, Bob received 201, while one-hundred-meter Olympic gold medalist Harrison Dillard came in second. (At Christmas in Tulare, Bob and Eugene had discussed the nomination but had agreed Dillard deserved to be the recipient.)

In February, Mrs. Mathias escorted her son to New York (Dr. Mathias could not leave his practice) to receive the award, where she expressed the humble appreciation of her family. Not one for long speeches, Bob said that the award was a great thrill, second only to the one received in London the previous summer. "I can only hope that I can live up to what this award stands for," he said, concluding his two-sentence acceptance speech.

Before leaving Kiskiminetas, Bob led his track team to a second place in the National Scholastic meet in New York City. In addition, he placed in the top twenty in his class academically, and he felt he was now ready for Stanford. Stanford agreed; he was promptly accepted, as was his friend Bob Hoegh. Together they would improve the football fortunes of the hapless red and white.

7

Hail Stanford, Hail

In the summer of 1949, Bob would have been content with his old job loading sacks of insecticide aboard crop-dusters. Instead, he trained with Coach Virgil Jackson, defended his National AAU Decathlon championship, and toured Scandanavia with a group of American athletes who competed in the "Little Olympics" in Norway.

On June 28–29, Mathias defended his national title on home turf at Tulare High Stadium, later to be renamed in his honor. The weather was better by far than it had been in both Bloomfield and London the previous summer. Competing on the home court didn't hurt either, and it showed in comparing Bob's respective point totals: Bloomfield, 7,224; London, 7,139; Tulare, 7,556. In comparing the Tulare performance to the one in London, Mathias bettered his marks in seven of ten events.

Later in the summer, Bob traveled to Oslo to compete in "The Little Olympics." Facing a strong field of international entrants, including Moon Mondschein and Billy Albans, he won the decathlon with 7,346 points. Having lost his "hard won" track shoes somewhere along the tour, he had to borrow a pair that were several sizes too small. Bob went on to take the gold medal anyway, but it was clearly a case of the thrill of victory and the agony of the feet.

The trip turned out to be a time for good-natured retribution. "I finally dished out to Moon some of the misery he had inflicted upon me during our cruise to the London games," Bob remembered. "Moon and Billy had apparently heard about my programmed method of relaxing, and thinking it might contribute to improved training, they mirrored my every move. Getting wise to their scheme, I decided to put them through a series of mad machinations. For example, I began each meal exactly on the hour or half hour. At night, I would get out of bed periodically to have a glass of water, or to take several deep breaths. Back in the sack, I could hear them jumping out of their bunks to do likewise. I had them bouncing in and out of bed like Jacks-in-the-box. On the surface, I was all business; inside, I was choking with smothered belly laughs." If Moon really had been trying to tire Bob on the way to London, as the youngster suspected strongly, Mathias had the last word.

Soon after the tour, Bob was off to Palo Alto. In spite of extensive recruiting pressures from dozens of universities, the "headhunters" had not prevailed. Scholarships of the most lavish sort were offered, but Dr. Mathias assured the suitors his son had long before made his decision to attend Stanford. The doctor let these other colleges know straight out that he concurred completely with his son's choice.

Even while Bob was in high school, coaches from all over the country had visited the young prospect. In fact, one day both the basketball coach and the football coach from the same school ran into each other in Tulare. Professional embarrassment was at a peak; the two admitted to each other that they were in town seeking the same prize.

During his first few days at Stanford, Bob spent a lot of time with Eugene, who convinced his "little" brother to concentrate first and foremost on school work. When Bob expressed an interest in medical school, he was warned that acceptance was no easy matter. (Gene himself would learn the hard way. In competition with returning Korean war veterans, he would fail to be admitted to medical school, and would decide instead to study hospital administration in Chicago.) Social pressures too, were great—from fraternities and sororities alike. Several fraternities vied for the internationally famous athlete. Invitations to sorority parties were plentiful and, it seemed, every other woman on campus had zeroed in on Bob as a target. Given these pressures, it was understandable that Bob elected not to play freshman football, though the decision proved to be a shock to much of the campus. They were anxious to see "Kiski's King Kong" in action.

Bob did allow himself one small extra-curricular diversion: he became a fraternity pledge. While Gene was a member of Sigma Nu, Bob chose Phi Gamma Delta, primarily because Tularean Bob Hoegh and several other close friends had elected to become "Fiji's," too.

From cleaning the floor with toothbrushes to bowing to upper classmen on demand, Bob proved quickly that he considered himself no better than any other pledge, and thereby won over other members as well as the other pledges. (Bob's secret for humility was simple: having long before learned the value of discipline, denial, and self-mortification, Mathias found no command or request, regardless how unreasonable, which could rival the regimen he had endured during his lonely quest for a medal in London.) As a tribute to his character and contributions, he would later be elected to the post of rush chairman, a position requiring judgement, leadership, and a good sense of humor.

Bob dated infrequently, but when he did, he usually took the young lady to a movie, than capped off the evening with dancing "in some quiet place." Remembering Gene's entreaties —books, books, books—he succeeded in discouraging any serious relationships, although he says he was mightily tempted a couple of times.

While he had triumphed, too, over the temptation to tackle freshman football, it was another matter when track season came around. Spring of 1950 had sprung, and this young man's fancy turned to thoughts of love—of track and field. Well rested now, he looked forward to strenuous activity, to competition, and, he hoped, to victory in the upcoming meets.

When he reported for track-and-field duty, a collective sigh of relief must have issued from all the Stanford rooters who were beginning to worry that Bob had decided to rest on his considerable laurels. On the contrary, he showed his talent and dedication from the outset. In his first meet he set freshman records in the discus, pole vault, high hurdles, and shot put. Stanford statistics indicate he was responsible for 28 of the 74 points that Stanford registered in this first meet against the rival California frosh.

He accumulated a total of 83 ⅓ points and averaged three gold medals in each of five dual meets during the track season, and was therefore in peak form for the 1950 national decathlon contest held in Tulare that summer. This meet proved to be his way of again saying thanks to his home town supporters with action rather than words, as he broke Glenn Morris' fourteen-year decathlon record of 7,900 points. In going beyond the record, Bob exceeded the 8,000-point barrier by a healthy 42 points, ran his fastest 110-meter hurdles thus far in 14.7 seconds, and set a new record of 13 feet ¾ inches in the vault.

Staying true to form, his first day of competition was good but not great. At sunset, Mathias trailed Billy Albans by a considerable amount. It was business as usual, however, on the second day, when the *wunderkind* not only overtook his friend, but exceeded his tally by 681 points. He was clearly prepared for the challenge of Helsinki.

A comparison of his 1948, 1949, and 1950 performances

in the national decathlon contest demonstrates his steady improvement leading up to his record-breaking performance in 1950:

Event	June 25–26, 1948 National AAU Decathlon Olympic Tryouts Foley Field Bloomfield, N.J.	June 28–29, 1949 National AAU Decathlon Tulare High Stadium	June 27–28, 1950 National AAU Decathlon Tulare High Stadium
hundred meters	11.2 sec.	11.3 sec.	10.9 sec.
long jump	21' 6⅝"	22' 4½"	23' 3⅜"
shot put	42' 6⅝"	45' 3"	47' 6¼"
high jump	6'	6' ¼"	6' ¾"
400-meter run	51 sec.	51.3 sec.	51 sec.
110-meter hurdles	15.1 sec.	15 sec.	14.7 sec.
discus	139' 7¼"	150' 11⅛"	146' 5"
pole vault	11' 6"	11' 6"	13' ¾"
javelin	157' 3⅜"	177' 10⅞"	182' 4½"
fifteen hundred meters	4:55.2	4:58.2	5:05
	7,224 points	7,556 points	8,042 points

Although thoughts of Helsinki might have occupied Bob in late June, in the fall, the concerns that governed his campus life were primarily academic. Again, he decided not to go out for football, electing rather to keep in shape on his own. Campus rumors had it that Bob was passing up football to avoid a serious injury that might interfere with his defense of the decathlon title in the summer of '52. While Bob denied it, no one could have faulted him for such a rational, practical decision. However, he would prove the rumors unfounded come the fall of 1951.

Despite a nagging back injury, he was once again a member of the Stanford track team in 1951. Unfortunately, the persistent back spasms he was experiencing prevented him from participating in the decathlon's ten events; instead he chose to concentrate on only three: the discus, hurdles, and shot.

Specialization generated desired results: a Stanford record of 173 feet 4 inches in the discus, an excellent shot put average of 51 feet 2 inches, and his attention to the hurdles would eventually generate his fastest time in the event—14.6 seconds —at the 1952 national decathlon meet.

His back spasms, plus the fact he had competed in only three events during the season, led him to toy with the idea of skipping the U.S. decathlon tourney that summer. An opportunity to attend one of the two required Marine boot camps (Bob was enrolled in the Marines' Platoon Leaders course) cinched the decision not to defend. "During the demanding basic training we underwent," he said later, "I thought often of the similarity between the Marine's hardships and those of decathlon training. Somehow, decathloning gets the best end of the stick."

In the fall of 1951, Robert Bruce Mathias finally reported for football practice. Having assaulted the books with the intensity and dedication of a true scholar, and still not attaining the high marks needed to get into med school, Bob decided he had little to lose by trying out for football.

Just as there had been skeptical reactions by the press after Bob won the Pacific AAU and U.S. decathlon titles in 1948, and just as the U.S. Olympic track coach and Coach Jimmy Marks at Kiski had taken a "show me" attitude, there was considerable coffee-cup coaching as to whether or not Bob could hold his own with seasoned members of the Stanford

Leaping high at Kiski.

Bob going around left end during a game at Stanford. He went on to lead the Indians to the Rose Bowl.

Entering the U.S. Marine Corps Platoon Leaders' Course at Stanford in 1951. (*Courtesy of USNAS Moffett Field, Calif.*)

Throwing the discus for Stanford.

Long jumping at the Helsinki Olympics in 1952. In this jump he sustained the leg injury that caused him pain throughout the meet.

Finishing the fifteen hundred meters in a time that gave him the championship and made him the first man to win two Olympic decathlon titles.

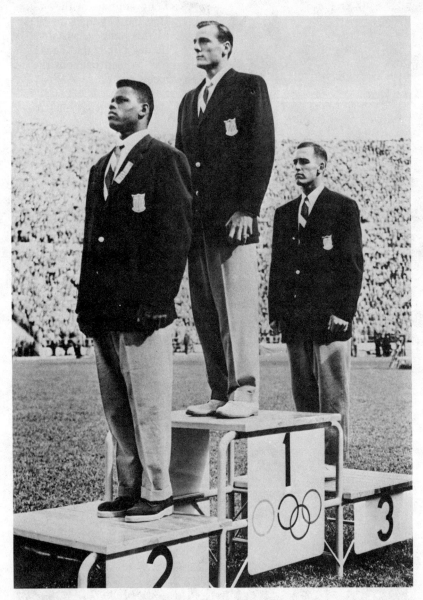

On the victory stand again. This time, all three medal winners are American —Milton Campbell, left, holds the silver, and Floyd Simmons, right, the bronze.

team, not to mention the opposition. "I must confess I had a couple of lingering doubts myself," Bob recalls. "It had been two years since football at Kiski; naturally I wondered if I could pick up the rhythm again. Besides, there were two veteran fullbacks returning to the team. At least Coach Chuck Taylor seemed to have no preconceived notions about who would start. This was his first year as Stanford coach, and lettermen were expected to re-prove themselves."

Doubting Thomases seemed at first to be right. In the first practice session, Bob was tentative, fractured a toe and failed to impress anyone. A week or so later, on his return to the practice field, he re-injured the toe, and on his third attempt, was slowed by an extremely sore thigh muscle.

"When I failed to make the travel squad for the first game with Oregon, I thought, 'Suppose the press turns out to be right. Have I become brittle in the two-year interim? Am I really meant to be just a track-and-field man, as some are saying, and should I be content with staying there?' From all directions, worried advisors were encouraging me to drop football to save myself for the 1952 Olympics." Bob reasoned, however, as he had done so many times before, that "You don't make a team by worrying." So he redoubled his efforts.

Stanford was not presumed to have much of a team, but managed to squeak by a weak Oregon eleven by a score of 27–20, and went on to beat San Jose by a 26–13 tally on the following weekend.

With toe and thigh recovered, Bob made the travel squad in time for the big game at Ann Arbor, against a menacing Michigan team. As a return man on kick-offs, Mathias ran the ball back twice, for seventeen and eleven yards respectively, thereby contributing in small part to the surprising 23–13 win over the Big Ten Wolverines.

While Coach Taylor was wrestling with the idea of switching Mathias to halfback for the UCLA game, both veteran fullbacks suffered injuries. Therefore, call it bad luck or good, Bob moved up to the first string fullback opening with less than a week of practice under his belt.

The next six games of the regular season are legendary around Palo Alto:

Stanford	21	UCLA	7
Stanford	21	Santa Clara	14
Stanford	14	Washington	7
Stanford	21	Washington State	13
Stanford	27	USC	20
Stanford	35	Oregon State	14

During the Oregon State game on November 17—his twenty-first birthday—Bob suffered an acutely painful hip injury. The bad hip kept him on the sidelines during the week of preparation for the coming game with California, which Stanford proceeded to lose, 26–7. Still, the Indians won the Pacific Coast Conference championship and a consequent bid to the Rose Bowl.

Still in pain, Mathias caught only one pass at the Rose Bowl, and the "Red Men," who had been playing over their heads all season long, thanks in large measure to Bob's leadership and spirit, were overwhelmed by Big Ten champ Illinois, 40–7.

It was a dismal conclusion to a sensational regular season, but for Mathias, the six UCLA-through-Oregon State games not only silenced the nay-sayers but turned them into avid supporters. His performances on the gridiron were remarkable. In his first game as a starter, he scored two touchdowns against UCLA. Against Santa Clara, two more TD's. In the game against the Washington Huskies, Bob helped set up the winning touchdown with a 33-yard gallop over tackle. On fourth down, with two yards to go from the five, Bob picked up three yards for a first down on the two. On the next play, the Indians racked up six points. In the ensuing battle with Washington State, Mathias averaged 4.5 yards on thirteen carries.

Next came the game with highly favored Southern Cal, during which Mathias showed additional versatility with a come-from-behind tackle of a runaway, punt-returning Trojan, which prevented what seemed to be a sure TD. Eugene Mathias was still not impressed. "Maybe, if Bob had had a few hurdles in front of him, he would have caught up with the would-be scorer sooner," was his comment.

With USC leading 14–7 in the fourth quarter, Mathias took a Trojan kickoff at his four-yard line and returned it through a myriad of defenders—stiff-arming, clawing, faking, and finally breaking into the clear on the sidelines for ninety-six yards and a touchdown. Lillian Mathias, meanwhile, was in the stadium and actually fainted in the excitement caused by her son's amazing run. The last man between Mathias and the goal line was Southern Cal's All-American quarterback and punter, Frank Gifford, who was left flat on the turf after Bob eluded his grappling attempt. When asked about the big play, Bob never fails to give credit to key blocking, especially by Wes Laubscher.

Stanford missed the extra point, leaving the score at 14–13, with USC ahead. An end-zone fumble recovery by the Trojans, followed by a flawed conversion attempt of their own, pushed the score to USC 20, Stanford 13.

Subsequently, a Stanford drive moved to the USC eight-yard line. In three carries, Mathias took it first to the five, over All-American Pat Cannamela; then the one; and finally into the end zone standing up. After the kick, the score stood tied 20–20. Before the final whistle was blown, Mathias proved invaluable in assisting with another touchdown to clinch a surprising 27–20 victory for the Indians.

In the dressing room, after the dust had settled, with the attending press gathering round the multitalented star, Bob began to remove the tape from his ankles. "Immediately, I realized I had forgotten to shave my legs before the game. Onlookers quickly gathered and roared with each moan and groan." Extremely embarrassed, Bob headed for the showers, thinking how quickly the thrill of victory can be lost.

In the following day's *San Francisco Examiner,* sports columnist Prescott Sullivan described the nature of the problem the Trojans faced on the game's biggest play:

> The Trojans might just as well have kicked off to Frank Merriwell or Tom Rover as kick off to Mathias in the action-packed fourth quarter, when they were only a touchdown ahead. It was a mistake, which must have sent recollections of their boyhood reading swimming before the Trojans' eyes.
>
> Mathias took the ball on his own four-yard line and ran it back 96 yards to a TD, even as Merriwell or Rover surely would have done. It just couldn't have happened any other way. Not in a game like this one, with the old school pleading for heroics. Bob Mathias, the Olympic decathlon champion, was born to save the day.

It was against Oregon State, before the damage to the hip, that Mathias had scored two more touchdowns and assisted in a third to lead the Indians in locking up the Pacific Coast Conference Championship, thereby assuring Stanford of the trip to the Rose Bowl. After that game, Coach Chuck Taylor said of one of Bob's touchdown runs, "I looked behind the path he ran and shuddered. Five Oregon State guys were stretched on the ground—all of them knocked groggy."

With Bob's injury would come the decline of Stanford's fortunes, but Mathias had silenced all the prophets of doom. Robert Bruce Mathias had proven his prowess as a college-class gridiron star, and he took all of the late-blooming press recognition with the poise of Gary Cooper at high noon.

In spite of injuries and a short season, he scored eight touchdowns, averaged 4.2 yards per carry, and 25.2 yards in kick-off returns. Not bad for a player who did not make the first team until the fourth game and who played at half speed during the last two.

With the season over, it was time to mend and begin thinking about a trip to Finland—and the 1952 Olympics.

8

A Man Doing a Man's Job

Bob's work for Helsinki began in earnest in early 1952, when he moved out of the fraternity house at Stanford and into an apartment without a telephone. The decision in favor of semi-seclusion was made for several reasons. "When you're in training, you need time to work, to think, and to rest," Bob maintained. "With the bustle of activity at the 'Fiji' house, not to mention the telephone calls, I didn't have enough time for any of the three, let alone my school work." It was a fact of life that with the fabulous football season he had played, Bob was now the co-ed rage; the fraternity house phone jingled day and night for him.

During the spring of 1952, Bob swam, played intramural basketball, and later reported for the Stanford track-and-field team's season. Coach Jack Weiershauser assured Bob he didn't expect him to participate in any events other than those of his choosing. He understandably didn't want to interfere with Bob's Olympic training, but the spirited young man offered to compete in whatever event the coach needed him.

A good beginning to the season was ensured when Mathias tested his previously painful back and found it to be spasm-free in the first meet. Entering four events, he won three firsts and a third place.

When Bob offered to run on the relay team as well, the coach declined courteously but emphatically. His point-maker was doing enough as it was. Against the Bears of California that day, the Stanford star won both hurdles events, the discus (as expected), and vaulted over 13 feet. He might have gone higher but declined to continue when the Indian victory was assured.

On the practice field, for his decathlon training, he concentrated as much as possible on his weakest events—those requiring running. It was imperative that he improve in the sprints and the fifteen hundred meters. The decathlon scoring system had been revised, giving the running events more weight and consequently favoring the smaller, faster Europeans, and for that matter, any smaller man. "They don't give points for worrying," Bob had said often, and he wasn't going to worry now. He had tried not to worry as a novice in London at age seventeen, so why should he begin as a twenty-one-year-old, established, experienced champion?

While he continued to perfect his on-the-field training, his off-the-field work also improved. His move to an apartment had paid off. There, he could work at his studies (his grades in his new education major rose to a solid B-average) and still have time to serve as campus representative for a major clothing manufacturer and make some much needed spare change. Before studying in the evenings, he relaxed with a book or at the piano. Sleep, of course, was no problem. It had never been. So, during that spring, Bob worked, thought, relaxed, and rested. At the training table, he partook of the basic foods which had helped him so much during his formative and competitive years.

In late June, he attended the NCAA meet at Berkeley, which also served as Olympic elimination tryouts for individual events. Qualifying in three of the events (high hurdles, discus, and shot put), Bob really did not have to exert himself. He was looking ahead to the National Decathlon rally to be held in Tulare on July 2 and 3, just over three weeks before the helter-skelter of Helsinki. Having been at Marine boot camp the previous summer, he was anxious to get back to decathlon competition.

There were 6,000 rompish fans in attendance as the Tulare festival began. Comparing Bob's marks in the 1952 National meet with the last time he had participated in 1950, one sees improvement in nine of ten events:

Event	June 27–28, 1950 National AAU Decathlon Tulare High School	July 2–3, 1952 National Decathlon Tulare High School
hundred meters	10.9 sec.	10.8 sec.
long jump	23′ 3⅜″	23′ 5¼″
shot put	47′ 6¼″	49′ 10⅞″
high jump	6′ ¾″	6′ 2¾″
four hundred meters	51 sec.	50.8 sec.
110-meter hurdles	14.7 sec.	14.6 sec.
discus	146′ 5″	157′ 11⅝″
pole vault	13′ ¾″	12′ 3¾″
javelin	182′ 4½″	193′ 10⅜″
fifteen hundred meters	5:05	4:55.3
	8,042 points*	7,825 points

For a change, Bob performed remarkably well on that opening day. So much so, in fact, that he broke Bill Albans' first day record of 4,385 points set in 1950. The twenty-one-year-old Stanford student totaled 4,394. In the pole vault, he failed to exceed his 1950 height of 13 feet ¾ inches. In all but two events, the vault and the fifteen hundred meters, he achieved his all-

*7,444 points using 1952 standards

time best; in the latter, he was off his best by 1/10th of one second. With this win, he also became the first man in history to win four AAU decathlon titles.

It was not an easy victory, however. Pushed by Milton Campbell in the four hundred meters, Mathias came in second but was 2/10ths of a second faster than his previous top tally. In the hurdles, he hit three of the sticks but managed a fantastic 14.6, which was 1/10th of a second better than his previous best. After fouling on his first attempt in the javelin, he rebounded with a world record throw of 193 feet 10 ⅜ inches.

Campbell came in second with 7,055 points. Floyd Simmons, third in London in 1948, ended up in the same bronze slot in Tulare. The trio would tangle again in Helsinki.

The Helsinki Olympics took place during a busy, uncertain time in world history—the Korean War was going on; internal conflict boiling up in Egypt would lead to Nasser's rise; a massive steel strike had broken out in the United States; and candidates and electorate were preparing for an upcoming U. S. presidential election.

For Bob Mathias, there would be good reason to remember the first half of 1952 as a period in his life marked by intense anticipation moderated by a heavy dose of press pressure.

In a way, there was much more pressure on Mathias to win at the Helsinki Games than there had been in London. In 1948, even the Olympic coach had not thought he could make it. Accordingly, Bob went into the games hoping for a bronze medal at best, and the experience necessary to do well in 1952. What he got was the gold, and the expectation of his supporters that he would compete and win in Helsinki. As the summer of 1952 approached, sportswriters across America were almost unanimous in the opinion that Bob Mathias was one U. S. team member who could be counted on to bring home a gold medal. It was a foregone conclusion.

Mathias said of the time leading up to Helsinki, "The fact that everyone expected me to win generated a fair measure of healthy pressure. In 1948, I was so young that I really didn't fully absorb the significance of the Olympics. I appreciated the fact that the games were some sort of humongous track-and-field meet, but because I didn't expect to place, I consequently felt a minimum of pressure. Actually, I would have been more than pleased to win a bronze medal.

"While I had put in only about one hundred days into training for the London games, the situation in 1952 was a different one altogether. Having worked long and hard in preparation, I had set for myself the goal of trying to break the record in total points with full cognizance that, with a victory, I would be the first person in history to win twice. In the four years since 1948, I had matured sufficiently to realize the full implication of back-to-back victories."

Press pressure or not, Robert Bruce Mathias showed up in Helsinki for the fifteenth running of the modern Olympics. "I found the stress in Finland was more than offset by the fun side of the games—that of getting to know people from different cultural backgrounds, often in spite of the impediment of a language barrier. In England, most of my pre-game time had to be devoted to working on unfamiliar events, but in 1952, I had the Stanford track season, the Berkeley NCAA/Olympic individual-event trials, as well as the National Decathlon meet under my belt. Of course, I was concerned, but I was not confronted by the maze of unknowns I had faced in 1948."

With that kind of experience, Bob approached the games with a feeling of moderate confidence, and he was able to enjoy mixing in a relaxed way with the people of the games and the citizens of Finland.

"Admittedly, I was particularly curious about the Russians. Because they had sat out the London Olympics, I knew little or nothing about them. Despite the rhetoric of the Cold

War and the difficulty our governments were having in communicating, I couldn't believe that, on a one-to-one basis, it would be impossible to relate on a friendly level."

There was a generosity of considerable proportion in Bob's attitude, considering that the Russians had been anything but congratulatory after his win in 1948. Soviet radio had labeled him a typically spoiled, exploited American youth. Calling Bob a "bum," the Soviet press boasted of an Estonian athlete, Heino Lipp, who, they claimed, could have outclassed Bob if the Russians had competed at Wembley.

Curiously, Lipp did not go to Helsinki, either. The Mathias threat might have been greater than they admitted, or perhaps they were concerned that the Estonian might opt for asylum. In any event, Mathias did not compete against him.

Politics aside, Bob soon was offered a visit to the USSR's training center at Otaniemi, and much to the consternation and dismay of some American coaches and fellow athletes, he accepted the invitation.

"The Soviet camp was six miles from the stadium; as I approached the entrance to the 'Little Iron Curtain,' as it was called, I was recognized by two Russians in sweat suits." Bob's photograph had been featured prominently in the pages of Finnish newspapers. No doubt, he was the best-known athlete at the Games.

"I immediately knew by the smiles on their faces that everything would be all right. Apprehensive at first, they were soon chewing the gum I offered. Their apparent pleasure convinced me I had made a hit with the Juicy Fruit. In turn, they offered cigarettes and cognac—hardly fare qualifying for my training menu, but the gesture of friendship was there all the same. I later wondered if they were trying to tempt me with a smoke and some booze to throw me off the training track, but I really don't think that was the case.

"Somehow, they made me understand they wanted to give

me a tour of their village. First, they led me to a large hall
decorated with Russian flags. Paintings of Stalin, Molotov, and
Politburo members were prominently displayed. Then, I saw
something strange to an American, but apparently a tradition
for the Soviets: a large assemblage of fancy cakes, one each for
the winners of gold medals.

"I assumed that the gigantic banquet table, replete with
caviar, fish, cheese, and vegetables flown daily from Leningrad,
was for officials, bureaucrats, and coaches. The main course of
thick steaks and potatoes was to follow. The shock on my face
must have been transparent when I saw the waiters pouring two
glasses of cognac and vodka for each plate. That was when I
began to realize that the athletic community is a privileged class
in a supposedly classless society; a privileged class, second only
to party officialdom.

"Surely, the incentive to excel is sharpened with the per-
quisites implied, if not pledged openly. Catering to the sense of
well-being of the athletes, officials had even brought along a
contingent of folk dancers, ballet companies, singers, and actors, performing on request.

"Between the Soviet and American facilities, there was a
marked disparity—with the plushness of their setup making
ours look spartan by comparison. While we lived in an atmosphere of basic necessities—concrete floors, plain bed, and
stools—they had fine furniture, carpeted floors, and a finely
appointed and well-equipped dining hall. Our dining room was
cold and drafty.

"However, there was one thing the Iron Curtain citizens
were clearly in short supply of—that priceless, intangible, inali-
enable right we so often take for granted: freedom. When I
invited my Russian friends to return the visit, they shook their
heads, replying disconsolately, 'Against regulations.' "

Bob, in contrast, walked the streets of Helsinki freely,
signing autographs, talking to youngsters, gladhanding athletes

from other nations. Little girls brought him cookies and cakes. Little boys followed the living legend around. As he touched the people and saw the warmth of their smiles, he thought of his newfound Russian friends in their posh surroundings. "I wouldn't have traded a minute of my time for all three and a half weeks of their stay."

In *Sport Magazine,* Mathias described the pre-Olympic fever in the Olympic village:

"There are always thousands of kids around the village, and they all want autographs. After signing a few hundred books, it's easy to brush the kids off or break the monotony by signing yourself as 'Bing Crosby' or 'Satchel Paige,' but if you're square with the small fry—if you really get interested in them—you'll discover they can open doors for you that make your Olympic trip twice as interesting. A couple of Finnish kids really educated me.

"The boy was ten; his sister thirteen. I thought they were pestering for candy and gum, as they kept hanging around, but finally, in broken English, they made me understand they wanted me to visit their house and meet their folks. They lived just a few blocks from our village, so away we went. . . .

"Pop was an ordinary workman—a mechanic—and their home, like mine, wasn't fancy. He and his wife spoke only Finnish; at first, the conversation was pretty futile, but the whole family was crazy about something they called '*Yleisurheilu,*' which turned out to mean track-and-field athletics. They had pasted up records of every great runner from Nurmi to Haegg. The mother served some tea and cakes, and the kids acted as interpreters. We had a wonderful, two-hour gab session in which I learned some local phrases.

"When I left, I could find out the price of anything I wanted to buy in Finland by saying '*Paljonko tama maksaa*' (How much does it cost?). Introductions I could now acknowledge with '*Hyvaa paivaa*' (How do you do). When a Finn said something nice to me, I could repay him with '*Kiitos*' (thank you). That, and some other words, came in handy and helped me make friends the next couple of weeks.

"One of our team attachés—a sober gentleman who made sure everybody kept in strict training—could have used an experience like that. Very straight-laced himself, he tried to order a meal in a Helsinki café. The waitress listened to his fractured version of her language, nodded, and went away.

"She came back and put down a bottle of gin on the table.

"If meeting the people on the street was great sport, observing the frivolity of Olympic athletes was even more hilarious. As they gather during the week to ten days before the games actually begin, the street scene becomes one of the most bizarre bazaars in the world. Although I never went in much for swapping, I enjoyed watching the unusual trades taking place.

"One of our weightlifters ran out of things to swap, so he cut off his shirttail and gave it to an Egyptian in exchange for the tassel on his fez. Then there was the Yugoslav who wound up with a girl's eyelash curler. He didn't know what it was for. When somebody told him, he paraded around with the curliest lashes this side of Max Factor's.

"Nylons, lipstick, and costume jewelry are very big items on the barter market, and you get back things like Swiss skiing caps, Russian kopeks, and Swedish jackknives. Some deals get real complicated. A bunch of Hungarians approached little Paula Jean Myers, the platform diver, but she couldn't understand a word they said. They began making snipping motions with their fingers. They pointed at her head. The way the swapping mania had hit the Village, almost anything went. 'Do they mean they want one of my ears?' Paula Jean wanted to know.

"But it was her pigtails they were after—and her pigtails they didn't get."

Soon it was time to stop visiting, swapping, and walking the streets. It was time to go for a second gold in the decathlon. On hand to help carry the Mathias family banner was Jimmy, who had also attended the London games. In the fall, he would enter Occidental College. There, like his brother, he would excel in the discus and shot put and eventually would be inducted into the Occidental Track and Field Hall of Fame. Like Bob, the discus would always be his favorite event. During his military service, he would place second in the discus as a participant in the United Allied Forces (in Europe) Games. Eugene was now in medical school at Stanford, having been admitted after graduating from the University of Chicago with a degree in hospital administration. Bob's father was too busy to attend, and Mrs. Mathias felt she should stay home with him and Patricia this time around.

While the press corps played up the threat of an unknown Russian team, Bob thought he knew who the real competition was: his powerful countrymen, Campbell and Simmons. Ignace Heinrich, too, posed a considerable challenge. Heinrich had come close—within a scant 123 points in London—and he looked to be in excellent condition.

Bob, however, was not overly concerned with the supposedly improved Heinrich. "Ignace and I became pretty good friends, having made our acquaintance four years previous in the mud of Wembley. We had the language problem whipped, what with Ignace knowing a little English and with my having had two years of French at Stanford. There was a natural kinship between us, fostered by our having placed one-two in the London games. So we practiced together, and I soon noticed that pole vaulting was a demanding event for the six-foot four-inch entrant. Literally, he almost knocked himself out every time he vaulted. If I had been Ignace, I would have skipped the event in practice. He was wearing himself out before the decathlon began."

Simmons was an opponent to be respected, having placed third in London, and having matured and acquired added experience in the interim. But Milton Campbell was the man to beat, Bob thought. He had really tested Mathias in the combined National Decathlon-Olympic Trials in Tulare in early July. Bob and he were friendly rivals, though: "I liked Milt Campbell the first time I met him. We kidded continuously. On the night before the Helsinki decathlon began, I chided him about going to bed early enough to be ready for the fifteen hundred meters two days hence. With a characteristic jovial reply, he advised me he would make so many points in the first nine events, he would be able to sit out the last one. Somehow, I think he half meant what he said."

The American decathletes had all the coaching and training help they needed. Brutus Hamilton, who had attended the 1948 games as an observer for the University of California, was now the coach of the U.S. team. Jack Weiershauser, Bob's Stanford coach, was present and available on an unofficial basis; several members of Hamilton's staff were also there to help.

In London, Hamilton had observed Mathias resting and relaxing under a blanket during the two-day storm. The coach went one better in Helsinki by having his people provide athletes with mattresses on which to lie down during the long delays between events. With twenty-eight participants at the opening, the schedule was sure to proceed more expeditiously than had the one with thirty-five entrants in 1948, but Brutus wanted his people to be comfortable just the same.

One of his people would be Simeon Iness, Mathias' friend and companion since childhood. Sim had persisted, and had made the team.

The days of festivity had now passed, and the time arrived for the decathlon to begin. It was time to get serious. Unlike his fantastic first day in Tulare on July 2, however, Bob returned to his usual form with a slow start.

"Like a schlemiel, I almost blew the whole competition at the beginning of the first event—the hundred meters. With my heart pounding in my ears, I mistook a loud click of a camera nearby for a misfired starter's gun, and took off in a false start. One more bad beginning and I would be disqualified—finis."

So Bob had to lay back on the second attempt to insure against potential disaster. It worked. Although he hit the tape at 10.9 seconds, 1/10th of a second slower than his Tulare time three weeks prior, he was first, and several yards—not feet— ahead of the supposedly ominous Russian duo of Volkov and Kuznetsov. They trailed with identical times of 11.44 seconds. Not a bad beginning, he thought; but one that surely would have been better had it not been for the false start.

In the long jump, Bob began to wonder if the cloud of poor luck that had followed him around on the first day in London had reappeared above Helsinki. His best jump was 22 feet 10.8 inches, which was much shorter than the 23 feet 5¼ inches he had jumped at the Tulare tryouts. What was more alarming was the flash of pain that shot through his left leg on his final and fruitless attempt to better the mark. He had just sustained what turned out to be an extremely painful pinched nerve in his hip. Reeling from the intensity of the pain, he nevertheless did not panic. He concentrated on staying calm, resisting the normal but futile reaction of wondering why such a thing had to happen at this crucial time.

In fact, to a certain extent, the injury helped to spur Bob's performance in the subsequent events. He thrived on adversity. He was best as a "come-from-behinder." A little heat, a brisk massage, an elastic bandage, and a bit of time to heal would be all he needed. As he would later say of Sim Iness, "You've got to have bedrock confidence." He did.

But there was more than the injury to test that confidence, as he pointed out sometime later: "It was a startling revelation when I learned that Volkov and Kuznetsov had jumped the exact same distance: 23 feet 3.12 inches, over four inches farther than I had achieved. Two events, two identical performances. Were these guys programmed? I had heard of Soviet central planning and control, but this was ridiculous."

When the contestants left the field for lunch, Campbell had the lead, having done well in both the hundred meters and long jump. After steak, potatoes, peas, and a quart of milk, Mathias felt restored, if not in perfect health. He felt that, though the injury was painful, he could deal with it better than the unexpected "official" setbacks he had endured in London. So far, his performance had been strictly up to him—and that's the way he liked it.

While the left hip was important in the shot put, the back, arm, and shoulder were more vital in the event. Bob managed to put his whole body into his toss, with the result a distance of 50 feet 2.37 inches. Coach Jackson's oft-repeated order to "explode" when projecting the metal sphere was demonstrated perfectly in Bob's attempt. It was his best shot ever in decathlon competition and good enough to put him in first place.

"In the high jump, I cleared 6 feet 2.81 inches and decided to withdraw from the event rather than chance further aggravation of the pinched nerve." It was a sound decision as this was already his all-time best jump.

Now it was time to take advantage of the mattress under the stands to get himself out of the drizzle and howling, biting Finnish wind. "Relax," he told himself. "Toes, feet, ankles, knees, thighs, hips—yes, especially the left one . . ." He slept until he was mustered out for the four hundred meters at 8:00 P.M.

Knowing he had a whole night ahead to rest the injury, he ran all out for an excellent 50.2 time, once again a personal best.

"Jimmy advised me that the time was good for 828 points; 42 above what I had earned recently in Tulare. He also told me Volkov was stalled at seventh place, while Kuznetsov was in twelfth. My compatriots, Campbell and Simmons, were second and third, respectively." Mathias was first, with a total of 4,367 points, only 27 behind his Tulare first-day total of 4,394, and remarkably good considering his shaky start and sudden injury.

The goddess of sleep was kind that night; but when Mathias awoke the thigh was stiff and painful. After breakfast, he went to the stadium for a massage and heat application before the 110-meter hurdles.

"The stiffened leg troubled me somewhat, but our trainer, Eddie Wojecki of Rice University, set me at ease by teasing me about the clump of red-brown hair that stood out from my otherwise sandy head of hair. My 'Fiji' fraternity brothers had dyed the shock while I was dead asleep one day after lunch."

After the rubdown and heat, an elastic bandage was applied, and the slightly lame competitor was as ready as he would be. Waiting for him on the track was a Finnish official, a slight man with a wide smile who offered to help Bob keep track of his score in relationship to the record. "I accepted gratefully. I needed all the help I could get.

"As we paced around waiting to be called to our positions, I thought of the hurdles event four years before, when Enrique Kistenmacher had tried to psyche me out by telling me he had it figured out that there was no way I could beat him." Enrique had hit the last hurdle and had never regained his lead.

This time, however, it was Bob's turn to hit a hurdle. "My 'heavy' leg caused me to alter my form slightly, so I hit the first hurdle and overran the others." Still, he was clocked in 14.7 seconds. The time was only 1/10th of a second under his outstanding 1952 Tulare time, and a full second faster than his London games time.

Pushing his countryman again, Milt Campbell beat Mathias with a 14.5-second run. When Bob inquired about Ignace Heinrich's time, he was informed that the Frenchman had dropped out due to a sprained ankle and back injury, the latter probably sustained in pole vault practice. "With Ignace out," Bob recalls, "Campbell was undoubtedly the man to beat."

Rain began to fall during the next event—the discus—and it must have seemed to Bob that a wet discus was standard operating procedure in Olympic competition. Despite the rain, Bob let fly with a fine throw of 153 feet 10 inches. It was over four feet shorter than his recent Tulare best, but 21 feet farther than Campbell, who placed second.

"I was standing aside, going over my scorebook, when I heard screams and gasping from the crowd. Looking up, I saw a discus hitting the turf nearby. I was later told a practice throw, gone astray, had almost trimmed my multicolored pate."

After lunch, which Bob had passed up in favor of a rub-down and rest, the pole vault competition began. In light of his difficulties in the long jump, hurdles, and the shorter-than-expected discus throw, he knew the coming event could determine whether he got enough points to break Glenn Morris' total points record, and, not incidentally, win himself another gold medal. Vaulting had never been easy for him, due to his large size and comparatively heavy weight. Today, it would be especially difficult for the 6-foot 2-inch, 199-pound man who also had to contend with a bum hip.

Slowest of all events to conduct, the pole vault went on for over five and a half hours, and delayed the javelin throw by three and a half hours. Daylight in Helsinki, however, was in generous supply. Wind blew, rain fell, and temperatures dropped, but the light remained until late.

When Bob elected to waive his turn in the pole vault until the bar reached 11 feet 1.86 inches, Eugene was not around, as he had been in Empire Stadium, to point out the potential pitfalls of the gamble. Again, though, his admonition would not have made a difference. Bob was even more uneasy than usual about the event. The two vaulting poles he had taken to Finland were the only two of their kind in the world. His favorite of the two—the one he had used in practice in the U.S.—had apparently been damaged in shipment. "Perhaps the glue used in its construction had dried up on the way to Helsinki. Whatever the problem, it broke during a practice session," Bob recalls. The ear-splitting sound of the shattering pole had made even Bob a little edgy. Now, all he had was the one pole to pull him through the event.

Missing on the first attempt, Bob sailed over the bar with dispatch on his second try, due at least in part to the help of his old coach, Virgil Jackson. For although Jackson was not in attendance, he was the one who had invented the glass pole to better accommodate bigger, heavier men like Mathias, and had persuaded a West Coast shipmast builder to produce it. It was now proving its worth. Using it for the first time in competition, Bob was able to clear the bar at higher and higher levels, until he surpassed the height of 13 feet 1.16 inches for his best effort ever, good for 745 points.

After Bob's final jump, the scorekeeping Finn told him he was 26 points off his world-record pace. So he decided to withdraw from the event for a rubdown and for a rest before the javelin, and after that, the last event—the metric mile. The Finn pointed out to Mathias that he could better his world mark—set earlier that summer in Tulare—if he threw the lance 195 feet and ran the 1,500 meters in 4.52 minutes or less. Heck, Bob thought, that's farther and faster than I have ever gone.

In warming up for the javelin, Bob remembers having trouble with his running approach. "As I concentrated on protecting my hip, I was neglecting other facets of my usual form. Coach Jack Weiershauser spotted my problem, but he wasn't allowed on the field, so he had to figure out an acceptable and effective way to let me know I wasn't following through after the throw. Quickly, he recruited a few American boosters and directed them to the end of the stadium nearest our position.

"My first two attempts were nothing short of lousy, and I was trying to analyze the problem when I heard voices from the stadium seats shouting in unison, 'Oh, Bob. Hey you. Don't forget to follow through.' Others who spoke English, and many who didn't, chimed in the chorus." Looking in the direction of the din, Bob saw Coach Jack leading the throng. "I gave him the OK signal and took my position for the next throw."

As it had in Wembley, the javelin streaked through the air, propelled as though it had another source of power besides Bob's own strength. In London, however, he had only reached 165 feet 1 inch. In Helsinki, with the help of the follow through, he sent the spear a distance of 195 feet 3⅛ inches, just slightly farther than the distance suggested by the Finn, and about 30 feet farther than he had thrown it in 1948.

Because he had exceeded 195 feet in the javelin, if he now ran the 1,500 meters in less than 4:55.3 he would break his own world record. That was exactly, to the tenth of a second, his time at the recent national meet in Tulare. Only once before (Bloomfield, 1948) had he run the race faster, but only by a tenth of a second. In London, where there had been more rain but where Bob did not have the painful leg injury he had here, his time was 5 minutes 11 seconds.

"I decided I would take it easy for the first half of the race to give the leg as little punishment as possible. If it was holding up, I would try to increase my speed for the last seven hundred and fifty meters. We had begun the day's first event at ten A.M. It was now ten P.M., a full twelve hours later.

"I was approaching total fatigue, but so was every other candidate in my heat. As testimony to our utter exhaustion, the popular Finn, Erkki Hautamaeki, in spite of applause and encouragement of the hometown crowd, collapsed in view of the finish line."

As Bob prepared to run his heat, darkness finally began to descend on the stadium. The main source of illumination now was the Olympic flame and the large scoreboard lights. At the start of the race, Bob wisely stuck to his strategy of running a relaxed first half, and his leg gave him little trouble. However, after two laps, when Mathias began to increase his speed, his leg began to hurt, resulting in his favoring his good leg and a limp that was visible even to spectators close to the event. With one lap to go, Mathias blocked the pain from his mind and pushed his tired body to its limit. With head up, chin out, teeth grinding, heels kicking buttocks, he conquered the last 375 meters by sheer courage and will power.

With his finish assured, one final question remained: would he cross the line in less than 4:55.3? The faceless crowd, concealed by darkness, cheered thunderously as Bob approached the finish line. His time, it turned out, was not the 4:55.3 needed for a new record, but rather 4:50.8; four and a half seconds faster than necessary to break the record and over 20 seconds faster than his London time.

His point total came to a remarkable 7,887—62 points higher than his previous world record. (A further revision of the scoring system would raise the total to 8,125 points, as periodically, the International Scoring Table is revised to more equitably balance points in relation to improving performances by recent athletes.) His first place total made him the first man in history to win the decathlon twice. (Eight Olympiads later, as the 1984 games in Los Angeles neared, this outstanding record would still stand.) His newfound friend, Milt Campbell, came in second with 6,989 points, some 898 points behind Bob. An Olympic bronze medal winner for the second time, Floyd Simmons finished with 6,785.

After finishing the race, Bob limped over to the bleachers, embraced Jimmy and said, "I wanted you to be the first to hear of my retirement." Then, while a horde of autograph-seekers headed in his direction, the grand old man of Olympic decathletes, at age twenty-one, made fast his retreat to the sanctity of the dressing room.

The world sports press had gathered there to meet him and they asked questions about how he felt, whether he expected to break the record, and whether he would compete again in Melbourne in 1956. Bob said that, except for his leg, he felt a great deal better than he had after the mud of the British Isles. As for breaking a record, he confessed that after the high hurdles of the previous day, he had felt he no longer had a chance at the record. His leg was hurting considerably. On the second day, during the pole vaulting, Bob had no doubt he wasn't going to break it. The hip had been aching terribly from the pressure imposed both from the approach and the jarring descent from a height of over 13 feet. His performance in the javelin, however, had put him back in the record-breaking groove, and he had then gone on to beat the required time in the fifteen hundred meters.

As to Melbourne, 1956, Mathias said, with certainty, "No." This was not an exhausted seventeen-year-old answering in the negative and then later reversing his position. This was a mature young man who had been through an immense amount in the past four years, telling reporters it was time for people like Milton Campbell to take over. As it turned out Milty would fulfill the prophecy and win in Australia, and Bob would be there, as a spectator, to watch him do it.

"Toward the end of the press conference, a Finnish official came in to tell me there were fifteen thousand people refusing to leave the stadium until they had a chance to cheer for me again; I went out on the track, ran a European-style victory lap, waved to everyone and received a tremendous roar in return. And then they began filing out. The Finns are great sportspeople."

On his way back to the dressing room, he found an ava-

In 1960, Bob carries the Olympic torch with old friend and teammate Sim Iness to help start the Olympic winter games, held in Squaw Valley that year.

Bob and his daughters (from left) Romel, Meagan, and Marissa, in 1965.

Bob has a lead role in *Theseus and the Minotaur*.

As Victor Mature's co-pilot in *China Doll*. Stuart Whitman is at center.

Congressman Mathias and Mrs. Shirley Temple Black, United Nations Ambassador, discuss the *Congressional Record* in his office in 1967.

Keeping in shape as a member of the Republican baseball team.

In 1968, Governor Reagan chats with Congressman Mathias.

Mathias wrist wrestles Jack Kemp. Donald Clausen, congressman from California, is the referee.

With President Ford, Bob's friend since they served together in Congress.

Bob and his wife, Gwen.

Bob's two Olympic gold medals. (*Jeff Killion, Gainsborough Studio*)

Running the track at the Olympic Training Center in Colorado Springs.

Five U.S. Olympic decathlon champions. From left, Bruce Jenner, Milt Campbell, Bob, Bill Toomey, and Rafer Johnson. (*courtesy of American Bell, Inc.*)

ing and throwing things can make an old man of
a guy."

Hamilton later was asked about Campbell's
chances of breaking Mathias' record some day:

"Maybe with three years of the kind of ex-
pert coaching Bob had," he said. "But it takes
something a little extra—a spark—and Bob has
it."

While millions of people around the U.S. woke up on
Sunday morning to such news stories about Mathias's triumph
and the Americans' domination of the event, the decathlon
award ceremony was taking place thousands of miles away in
Helsinki.

As in London, the Helsinki competition had ended quite
late on a Saturday night, so late, in fact, that the Finnish band,
which was charged with playing the national anthems for the
new Olympic winners, had departed for the evening. Therefore,
the victory ceremony was postponed to Sunday.

Bob vividly remembers his feelings on the victory stand:
"In London, I was proud as punch that two of us on the
platorms were Americans; but I couldn't help but feel compassion for Ignace Heinrich of France who had placed second. He
had done well, but here he was, standing at attention, listening
to *my* national anthem.

"Here, in Helsinki, we didn't have that problem. All three
winners were from the greatest country on the globe. I tell you,
it was a magnificent moment."

In Tulare, the celebrating began on Saturday afternoon
and carried on into Sunday, as had happened during Bob's
Olympic victory four years earlier. Only this time, as the only
town in the world with two 1952 Olympic gold medalists, there
was an even greater cause for jubilation.

Bob's friend, and past competitor, Simeon Iness, had done it, too. He had taken the gold in the discus. Not even New York City, London, Paris, or Moscow could boast of two 1952 gold medalists. Tiny Tulare could and did.

Mathias described his deep feelings of pride in Sim's accomplishment to *Sport Magazine*'s Al Stump:

"As long as the Olympics are held and I'm around, I'll think of Sim Iness. Back at Tulare High School in California, Sim didn't get the breaks I got. He finished sixth, and out, in the final team trials; if he seemed to be a choked-up guy when he saw me off, I could readily understand it. It's a long time between Olympic Games, and usually you don't get a second chance.

"But Sim wouldn't let go of his dream. He has competitive Cherokee Indian blood in him, and he made the team in 1952. Then, at Helsinki, he uncorked a discus throw that won him a gold medal, beat the defending champion, and set a new Olympic record. Sim weighs 245 and stands six feet six inches, but he was floating on air right then. I'll never forget the cablegram he sent his wife, Jeane, in Los Angeles: 'We did it. I love you 1,000 times. Distance 180 feet 6.58 inches.'

"Sim said 'we' because nobody wins an Olympic title alone: it's a team accomplishment all the way. In that cablegram, he told Jeane what every woman wants to hear, plus how happy he was to win for her and the folks at home. Mentioning the distance was Sim's pride speaking. If you don't have pride in your ability—bedrock confidence—you'll never make it to the top."

It was soon after lunch on Saturday that the word was received in Tulare. Immediately thereafter, delirious dancing and impromptu parading began in the streets. Cars, trucks, bicycles, and farm tractors participated. Smoke bombs were detonated, creating an eerie make-believe effect in the usually calm and quiet town center.

Posters, placards, and banners soon were put up saluting the two hometown heroes. Dr. and Mrs. Mathias were at the Tulare Hotel, where a teletype had been installed for late-breaking information. Always the more demonstrative of the two, Lillian broke down on hearing the news of the victory, saying, "It's simply wonderful. I just knew he would come through—even if he had to do it on one leg." The lady, who had told her son in London, "never again, it's too hard," had not tried to dissuade Bob once he had made up his mind to defend his Olympic title. Now she was elated; elated he had won again, but just as relieved that it was all over. Together, the proud parents led a parade of their own, strolling arm-in-arm through the streets of the little town—the little town the good doctor had called "pretty near the perfect place to raise a family," the first time he had seen it. Turning to Lillian during the parade, Charles said in his typical understated way, "I guess Robert did quite a day's work."

Across the Atlantic and lying in bed later that victorious Saturday night and early Sunday morning, Bob couldn't relax, or maybe he didn't want to. The storm of competition had passed, but the excitement had not subsided. Reflecting on the last four years and one hundred days, he remembered the highlights: a surprising win in Pasadena; repeating at the National Olympic Decathlon tryouts in New Jersey; the rain and the rewards in London; the quiet days at Kiski; defense of his title in Tulare in 1949, 1950, and 1952; football at Stanford in the interim; and now, this amazing time in Helsinki.

When his thoughts drifted to family and friends in Tulare, as they always did sooner or later, he tried to imagine what was happening back home. Images of caring, smiling, supporting friends and family moved through his consciousness, until, with those serene images in mind, Tulare's first citizen finally drifted off into relaxation and triumphant sleep.

9

Olympics to Olympics: Helsinki to Colorado Springs

November 17, 1977: Robert Bruce Mathias is forty-seven years old. It is now a quarter of a century since he stood the sports world on end by becoming the only man in history to win the Olympic decathlon for a second time, and doing so in record-breaking fashion.

A little heavier now, but still trim and handsome at 6 foot 4 inches and weighing 215 pounds, Bob has not been dealt a bad hand by Father Time. Quick-witted, ebullient, friendly, and always modest—this is essentially the same Mathias who took his second gold in 1952. On this particular birthday, Bob is exceptionally busy. The United States Olympic Committee has assigned to him the task of repairing and renovating an old Air Force facility in Colorado Springs.

It's a tall order. Mathias has been at the base since June of this year, when he was appointed Director of the U.S. Olympic Training Center. Its mission: to give America's amateur athletes a headquarters for year-round training during the four-year period between the Olympic games.

On mornings like this one, Bob is tempted to question his

judgment at having accepted the responsibility. There is staff to be hired and trained; construction to be supervised; the media to keep informed; and a budget to be adhered to. In addition, a group of hockey players is arriving within days.

Finally, it is noon. Closing the office door, Mathias puts his feet up on his desk, relaxes, and, in classic Olympic style, goes to sleep. The trip from Helsinki to Colorado Springs, has been demanding at times, but Bob has not been anxious. He still knows the importance of well-timed cat naps and relaxation.

As we look back to the period following the Helsinki victory, we see Bob returning to Stanford, and graduating from there in the spring of 1953. After receiving a temporary deferment from the Marine Corps, he began planning for a movie that Hollywood wanted to make of his life, entitled, appropriately, *The Bob Mathias Story,* and starring Bob as himself.

The movie was filmed in early 1954 in Hollywood and on location in Tulare. A United Artists release, the movie was shown in packed movie houses from California to Broadway. Moviegoers had heard and read of Bob's feats; now they could see a recreation of the events leading up to, and including, the Olympic victories in 1948 and 1952.

The shooting of the film was completed just in time for June nuptials, starring Melba Wiser of Modesto, California, and Bob Mathias. They had met at Stanford and together had been announcers on a campus radio program. As if to compensate Lillian, who "so wanted a daughter" when Robert was born, the Mathias couple would have three children and all would be girls.

The newlywed entered active service in the U.S. Marine Corps as a second lieutenant at Quantico, Virginia, in July 1954, and served there for six months until his transfer to Camp Pendleton, California. Besides serving in an infantry training unit, he spent several months as a member of an underwater demolition team, where again his sizeable feet were an asset in propelling him through the water.

Twice during his Marine Corps hitch he was tagged by the State Department for four-month goodwill tours that took him around the world. As a representative of the Amateur Athletic Union, and on an eventual total of five trips abroad for the State Department, Bob would organize, encourage, and promote sports and youth programs on five continents. And, according to Virgil Jackson, Bob scored more points in nine events in a Marine decathlon competition than he had ever amassed in all ten.

On March 16, 1955, Bob and Melba's first daughter, Romel, was born.

Following military service, Mathias went back to Hollywood, where he worked for John Wayne at Batjac Productions from October 1956 to April 1958. In November 1956, while working for "Duke," he was off again on another goodwill trip for the State Department, during which he attended the Olympic Games in Melbourne, Australia, as President Eisenhower's personal representative.

Bob remembers Melbourne: "Also attending as the president's representative was Dr. Sammy Lee, a 1952 Olympic diver. He was about five feet two inches tall while I reached six feet four; we looked like Mutt and Jeff as we covered Melbourne from one end to the next. As envoys of the U.S. Government, we were given 'royal' treatment by the hospitable Aussies.

"It was a genuine pleasure for me to see the games for the first time from the vantage point of a spectator. As I watched the decathlon competition, I became extremely involved, knowing all along what the contestants were thinking, feeling, fighting.

"When my friend, Milt Campbell, won, I was overjoyed. His unrelenting pursuit in Finland had contributed to my breaking the record. Now it was a real kick to see him pushing someone else and finally standing on the winning platform himself."

Prior to the trip "down under," Bob had considered making a comeback in the Melbourne games. In the previous winter, he had made a speech in which he warned that Russia would soon dethrone the U.S. as the preeminent team in track and field. "Still in pretty good shape, I felt we would need every point we could get, and so I wanted to 'unretire.' But I inquired about my amateur status, and my request for reinstatement was summarily rejected on the grounds that I had earned income from endorsements resulting from my athletic career."

It would have been interesting to see if the twenty-five-year-old Mathias could have gone against the odds again. What he had done at seventeen and twenty-one, he just might have repeated at twenty-five. Virgil Jackson, for one, is convinced he could have done it again. "Why, at Stanford, he threw the discus 170 feet and, in Switzerland, he ran the hurdles in 13.8 seconds," the coach proclaims.

In any case, after Melbourne, Mathias went back to the States and acting. His career had a boost in 1957, when, as Victor Mature's co-pilot in *China Doll,* he flew C-47s over the Burma Hump. Also in that year, the number of children in the Mathias family doubled when Megan arrived on October 12.

In 1959, Mathias did six months of training with a worldwide construction firm for his role as Keenan Wynn's protege in a construction/adventure television series called "The Troubleshooters," which lasted only one season. Still, the close association between the two actors nurtured a warm friendship that would endure and grow through the years.

In 1960, Bob, Melba, Romel, and Megan were off to Rome as Dad played the lead role in *Theseus and the Minotaur.* Bob enjoys telling unsuspecting interviewers that he played the part of the Minotaur, a creature from Greek mythology with the body of a man and the head of a bull. Surely Mondschein, Kistenmacher, Heinrich, Vlokov, and Kuznetsov could have been convinced of this. In reality, of course, Mathias played Theseus, King of Athens, who slew the Minotaur.

Conveniently, while in Rome, Bob attended his fourth Olympic Games, where he was the color commentator for one of the U.S. networks.

"With the atmosphere of ancient times so pervasive, the color and excitement in Rome were extraordinary," he remembers. "For example, the marathon was held along the Appian Way, the ancient Roman military road dating back to 300 B.C. Other events were conducted in some of the old outdoor theaters and, with the ruins of the Roman Forum and the Colosseum standing as sentinels, the city made you feel as if you were back at one of the ancient games. Rafer Johnson of the United States won the decathlon with a new record of 8,392 points; our friendship and association continue to this day."

After the Rome games, while continuing his acting career, Mathias crossed the Mediterranean to Greece, the birthplace of the ancient tournaments, to play opposite Jane Mansfield, "the blonde bombshell," in *It Happened in Athens*.

In 1961, on May 22nd, the Mathiases welcomed Marissa, their third daughter, into the world. Bob spent that year doing commercials, making speeches, endorsing products, and making plans to open two youth camps in the Sierra Nevada mountains of California. The two facilities—one for boys, one for girls—opened in 1962 and continued under his direction until 1978, when the operation was sold.

In 1964, Bob attended the Tokyo Olympics, his fifth Games in a row—two as a participant, three as a spectator.

"Deciding to attend the games in Japan as a last-minute thing, I missed my late-evening flight and arrived after the opening day ceremonies had concluded. Finding hotel accommodations and tickets were like finding a grain of rice in a

Sapporo snowstorm." Bob finally succeeded but not before being somewhat taken aback by the sight of the millions who had crowded into the already crowded Japanese capital. However, Bob remembers that "in spite of the multitudes, organization of the games was nothing short of excellent; the detail-oriented Japanese built freeways to move the throngs, left no teahouse unscrubbed, no kimono unwashed, and no sake unpoured."

Bob's interesting and varied career took a dramatic turn in 1966. From the peaceful world of running the Sierra Nevada Camps, his ambitions turned to politics. "Primarily, I ran for Congress from California because I thought I could contribute. Secondly, I must confess, I enjoyed the competition."

Compete, he did. When the election results were in, he had unseated a fourteen-year congressional veteran. As a "fiscal conservative," Bob was re-elected three times and served for a total of eight years. During his tenure, he was on the House Foreign Affairs and Agriculture committees and was a delegate to the House NATO Conferences.

In 1974, a lean year for some fifty-six Republican incumbents with the tremors of Watergate and Nixon's resignation being felt by all in the party, Bob was defeated. Victim also of a reapportionment of his district, Bob watched helplessly as he lost much of his constituency.

"No one likes to win more than I do, so my defeat was a bitter pill to swallow. However, once I realized that you can't win every time, the loss became easier to accept. Finally, even in losing, I found something positive. If that had not happened, I probably would never have become as actively involved in the Olympic movement as I am today. I believe everything happens for the best, although sometimes I believe you have to help 'everything' along. This golden opportunity sustains that belief."

Of his congressional career, he says, "Eight years was

enough. Although I learned a lot and still feel it was a good experience, I wouldn't want to try it again." Bob regrets the fact that his party was in a congressional minority during his four terms of House service. "Politics can be very frustrating, particularly if you are on the minority side, as I was. No matter how good your ideas are, they make no difference if you can't get them across. In our political system that is sometimes impossible, unless you're willing to sell your soul. It's like playing football with eleven men on your team and thirty-three on the other," he said. "You're forever running into a stone wall."

One of Bob's pet projects in Congress was a "bill of rights" for athletes, giving an individual athlete recourse to appeal to an impartial body if penalized by any of the ruling amateur athletic groups. In 1978, Congress saw the wisdom of the proposed legislation and enacted it into law. "I believe this statute will affect the future of amateur athletes in a positive fashion for generations to come," he says. The law is known as the Amateur Sports Act of 1978.

Keeping his attendance record intact, Bob traveled to the 1968 Olympic Games in Mexico City and the Munich Olympics in 1972.

"In 1968, I was invited to attend the Mexico City Games by the Mexican Olympic Committee and, as a result, I was given the red-carpet treatment by public leaders and game officials alike. The newly completed track-and-field stadium at the University boasted the best-looking track I had ever seen.

"During the two days of decathlon watching, my pulse quickened by several beats as I again found myself on the field in spirit. Throughout the proceedings, my legs twitched continually during the jumping events, arms strained during the weights, and my breathing accelerated as each race began. I was exhausted by the time American Bill Toomey, a phenomenal athlete, was declared the winner.

"Of course, when I recall the Munich Olympics, I can

never erase the thought of the brutal massacre that will unfortunately live on in infamy.

"I still agree with the decision of the Olympic officials to continue the games. That's what the Israeli officials wanted. Besides, termination was exactly what the terrorists who killed the Israeli athletes were seeking."

President Gerald Ford, in early 1975, appointed Mathias Deputy Director of the Selective Service. He served in that capacity until August of that year, when he resigned to become State Financial Chairman on the President's Election Committee.

In the following year, he, of course, attended the 1976 Olympics in Montreal, this time as a representative of *Sports Illustrated*. "Although there were major organizational problems [like an unfinished stadium], the pageant was enjoyable for me, especially with the ease of communicating in English."

The color, pageantry, and global representation evident in the opening and closing ceremonies reflected the phenomenal growth the Olympics had undergone in the short time since Bob's first participation in the movement in 1948.

"In London, there must have been no more than four or five thousand participating athletes from about sixty countries. Twenty years later, there were ten thousand athletes from over one hundred countries. Baron Pierre de Coubertin would have been proud . . . as proud as I was when another American, Bruce Jenner, won the decathlon with 8,618 points . . . another new record."

During that year of 1976 and part of the next, Mathias served on the President's Council on Physical Fitness—until the call came from the U.S. Olympic Committee.

In mid–1976, after twenty-two years of marriage, Bob and Melba separated, so Mathias was a single man when he arrived in Colorado Springs in 1977.

"Although I wish to emphasize I am in no way complaining, my life has often been pulled in many directions. In so many ways, my life has been a decathlon. The political portion of my career was my decision, but not entirely my idea of the quiet, peaceful, relaxed life I like to lead. I get calls daily from people who want me to get involved in this cause or that, in one venture or another. I have been offered jobs of almost every description, but the opportunity and stability afforded by the USOC position were welcomed without hesitation."

While his position requires long hours on the job, Bob has not left the field of active participation in sports. He skis in Jerry Ford's Celebrity Cup in Vail, plays tennis in Alan King's Classic in Las Vegas, swims, plays golf, and stays in excellent shape. Not bad for a guy who is losing a few strands of sandy hair to gray.

Some say he's a natural athlete in everything he tries, a claim that will not be disputed by his golfing partners, who saw him break into the 80s on his second or third round. As the leader of a Springspree Superstars team in 1980, his group won the gold medal. In a television superstar competition for retired athletes, Bob came in fifth, in spite of the fact that many of the contestants were many years his junior and only recently retired from professional sports. And with speed skater Eric Heiden, decathlete Rafer Johnson, cyclist and speed skater Sheila Young Ochowicz, and gymnast Cathy Rigby, he serves on Southland Corporation's Olympia Awards Selection Committee, a program that recognizes and encourages outstanding American amateur athletes.

Nowadays, however, his primary interest—his true love— is the Training Center. Here, he helps make it possible for America's youth to have a better opportunity to compete against athletes from countries whose Olympic programs are supported with direct governmental subsidies. Here, he helps young people realize their potential and enchance their physical and mental talents in the arena of athletics.

It is interesting to follow Bob around the USOTC campus. Although he seldom eats lunch (another idiosyncrasy in his inventive health habits), he visits the huge dining room almost daily, where he rubs elbows with past and future Olympians. Some of the newcomers don't know Bob Mathias, especially those outside the world of track and field. After all, many of their parents were in elementary school when the high school graduate stunned the world in 1948. It is entertaining to see their reactions when someone tells them, "He did what Bruce Jenner did, except he did it twice. And he was only seventeen when he did it the first time." Bob usually adds, with a twinkle in his eye, "Back in the good old days, I was what you might call a 'poor man's Bruce Jenner.' "

(Bob's own comparison of himself to Jenner brings up an interesting, and inevitable, comparison between the living U.S. decathlon champions. To sum up their particular talents briefly: Jenner's outstanding achievement was the result of perhaps the best preparation of any of the champions. Toomey was a quarter-miler first—an excellent runner who overcame his under-average size (for a decathlete) to win in style. Rafer Johnson's specialty was the long jump, and he built on it to break the record. Strong, tenacious Milton Campbell was a specialist in the high hurdles. All of these men have made their memorable marks in different ways. Looking farther back, there is also the great Jim Thorpe to consider, who won the decathlon in 1912. Bob Mathias is probably the most extraordinary athlete of them all, though, having accomplished what he did with such little preparation and yet with such grace in 1948, and with such tremendous results in 1952. It is remarkable to think that, of the ten decathlon competitions Bob entered in his career, he won them all.)

Unquestionably, athletes are not the only people at the Center who admire and are impressed with Bob. In following him around the facility, one sees that every one of his people

—from janitor to manager—receives a greeting, which is returned warmly. Always gregarious, Bob relates to friends, staff, and neighbors on a close, caring basis. A recent acquaintance of Bob's was moving into Bob's neighborhood one day, when the phone rang in the neighbor's house. It was Bob Mathias. "Hey, you need a strong back to help you unload?" Stammering, the neighbor-to-be thanked him, told Bob he had it under control and hung up, astounded. "That Bob Mathias is for real," he declared to his wife.

A girl at Stanford said it best, however: "Bob Mathias is a somebody who thinks he's a nobody." Another friend maintains, "I would like Bob Mathias even if he had been second-string center on Tulare High's basketball team, or if he had placed fourth in the discus at the Fresno Relays, or even if he had fumbled the ball during his return of Frank Gifford's punt in that glory game between Stanford and USC. He's that kind of a guy."

As one might expect of someone who has kept his love of simple pleasures despite a sometimes complicated, often public life, many of Bob's happiest moments find him planting and manicuring shrubs, nursing the grove of aspens he planted in the front yard, treating the lawn, or repairing the driveway. On as many weekends as possible, Bob, Gwen, (his wife since 1977), and stepdaughter Alyse head for "a little patch of heaven" they own in the mountains above Colorado Springs. Bob has plans to build a small cabin on the property someday. Gwen, who is an attractive, friendly woman with a lyrical southern accent, talks of the need sometimes to retreat to their mountain home: "We need to get away from the hustle and bustle of the city and our respective jobs." The Forrest City, Arkansas, native—owner and manager of an interior design firm in the Springs—says her husband "goes to Greece, or Tokyo, or Rome like I go to Safeway, and I go along with him as often as I can, so we need the quiet times. I like nothing better than to see him enjoying serene hours angling on a mountain stream. Trout fishing is still one of his favorite pastimes."

Bob's travel itinerary includes as many visits as possible with his three grown daughters, who are scattered across the country from California to Texas. Of course, he also travels often to his hometown, his favorite place in all the seven continents (he's seen them all), to keep tabs on his "middle-aged" parents, his brothers and sister, and on "Mathiasville, U.S.A."

Dr. Mathias is now retired, and Eugene, also an M.D., is engaged in general family medicine, with a specialty in obstetrics. Jimmy is Maintenance Director of Three Rivers School near Tulare, and Patricia is Director of Budget and Special Project Coordinator at Kaweah Delta Hospital in Visalia.

In 1977, Tulare County renamed its newly renovated stadium "Bob Mathias Stadium" in festivities that lasted the greater part of a week. Bob could not have been more pleased if the British had renamed Empire Stadium in Wembley after him. It was a joyous occasion, one with pleasing echoes of past competitions won, high school records broken, medals earned (mostly gold), and three successful defenses of the National Decathlon championship, all in that same facility.

Robert stays in touch with his Tulare coach, Virgil Jackson, who is retired and living in Green Valley Lake, California. Jackson affirms his feelings for his pupil: "Over the years, Robert has been gracious in remembering." He points proudly to a picture of a July fishing trip when thirty-five barracudas were caught. "When the State Department needed a coach to visit and participate in Tunisian and Ethopian coaching clinics, Bob recommended me. He came to the Newport Beach YMCA annual banquet as principal speaker when I was serving as president of the organization. When I was head of a state fairs committee, Robert was there to present trophies to the winning organizations. And when the Royal Canadian Mounties performed at the Los Angeles County Fair, Robert was there at my behest to take the salute from the troops. Yes, Robert has been most gracious in remembering."

Due to the troubled international political scene in 1980, the United States Olympic team did not participate in the Moscow games. Although he did not agree with the Olympic boycott strongly advocated by President Jimmy Carter, Bob Mathias did not attend the Olympics—the first time since 1948 that he had not been present. "The Olympic Games represent the strongest moral force in today's society," Mathias wrote in the *Washington Star* at the time immediately preceding the boycott. "All of us abhor the violation of human rights in the USSR. All patriotic Americans would like to see a redress of conditions in [that country]. I am one of the loudest to decry the actions of [Russia] in invading Afghanistan; [its] actions . . . are irresponsible. However, despite the gloom along the international front, there is still no reason to involve sports, particularly the Games."

Mathias quoted Avery Brundage, for many years president of the International Olympic Committee: "If we canceled the Olympic Games every time there was an international disagreement, we would never get to hold them."

Time has not dampened Bob's strong feelings on the subject. On a 1983 radio program for the Mutual Broadcasting System, Mathias reiterated his conviction that "politics is poison" to the Olympic movement. He is also fully convinced that a larger percentage of the American people now share his views on the controversy than was the case in 1980.

The anti-boycott column Mathias wrote for the *Star* would be added to a voluminous collection of clippings compiled by Lillian and Charles Mathias. In 1982, the Bob Mathias archives, a 543-piece collection, were moved from the Mathias home. Trophies, medals, tattered uniforms, covers of national magazines—even small bottles containing soil from world-famous stadia—all went to a new home in the Public Library to be displayed until the Tulare Historical Museum is built.

While it was difficult for curators Charles and Lillian Mathias to get accustomed to the emptiness of their home after the move, relocation of the memorabilia came at a most appropriate time. During that same year, Bob's mother suffered a major heart attack, endured by-pass surgery, and fought valiantly against a lingering, post-operative case of hepatitis. Lillian, as much the fighter of odds as her famous son, won all three battles of that health war handily, although she complains with tongue-in-cheek about one persisting problem: "I sometimes think when they put me on the heart-lung machine, they by-passed my brain. I just don't remember so well anymore."

Actually, Lillian remembers the important highlights well enough—such as reading to a sickly son, or standing on the front porch and blowing her whistle at evening to alert the kids to dinner, or organizing the brood for a weekend trip to the mountains. She remembers very well the time she failed to recognize her son in a hurdles race because he had bleached his hair; she recalls the exhausted new U.S. decathlon champion calling from New Jersey to ask for a ride from the airport, and she can hardly forget her heart "almost bursting" with pride as Robert stood on the winner's platform in London as the band played his national anthem. Although the memories run one into the other, she can recollect witnessing in person the three successful defenses of Bob's national decathlon crown, and proudly escorting her son to receive the coveted Sullivan Award. And she will always remember the tape ticking away the news of the record-breaking victory in Helsinki.

It is now over thirty years since the Helsinki triumph, but the honors keep accumulating for Mrs. Mathias' son. In 1983, Robert was selected as one of the twenty charter members of the U.S. Olympic Hall of Fame, joining other immortals such as Jesse Owens, Mark Spitz, Jim Thorpe, Eric Heiden, Al Oerter, Babe Didrikson, Wilma Rudolph, John Weismuller, Rafer Johnson, Don Schollander, Bob Beamon, Dick Button, Cassius Clay (Muhammed Ali), Bob Richards, Harrison Dillard, Peggy Fleming, and Eddie Eagan. There is indeed so much for Mrs. Mathias to remember. But be patient, Lillian. There is still more to come!

As this book was going to press, Bob Mathias was appointed Executive Director of the National Fitness Foundation. In cooperation with the President's Council on Physical Fitness and Sports, the Foundation will establish The National Fitness Academy in Indianapolis to promote a high level of physical fitness and sports participation by all Americans.

AFTERWORD

As I put my name to these final pages, I can't help but find myself reflecting upon my own experiences as a young athlete, comparing them with what we are able to offer to the Olympic hopefuls of today. What dramatic changes have occurred in just a few years, and what an exciting time it is to be involved in the Olympic movement in America.

Just now a group of weightlifters passed my office window on their way to another workout—perhaps their third for the day. Some of them have been here at the Olympic Training Center for over two years. At the main gate to the Olympic Complex some twenty-or-so cyclists, including a current world champion, have left for what is probably a twenty to thirty-mile trek into the mountains lying west of the Center. Shooters, wrestlers, race walkers, and boxers are among other athletes here—all of them training, day in and day out, for the chance to represent this great nation and its people at future Olympics. They're representative of the more than one hundred athletes currently in residence at the U.S. Olympic Training Center. For the time being they'll call Colorado Springs home as they prepare themselves physically and mentally to compete for coveted positions on our Olympic teams. Throughout the year they're joined on and off by more than a thousand others, some of them the best in their respective sports, others working their way up, all of them sharing in the same dream.

Working with these young athletes as I do every day fills me with pride and encouragement. They're special and, I'm sure, will have great things to contribute to America long after their athletic careers are over. Speaking personally, they recreate for me those magic times, special feelings, and personal triumphs that led up to my Olympic gold medals in the decathlon in 1948 and 1952. One day one of them may break that record. How well I can identify with what they've set as their goal. Admittedly, it's difficult not to live vicariously through their drive and ambition to be the best. Almost daily they perform at levels considered astounding in my day. How often I wonder how I would fare in the tremendously competitive environment in which they find themselves, fighting for those relatively few spots on the Olympic team.

The idea of Olympic hopefuls coming together like this to live and train together—with the best coaching and with all the advantages that this technically advanced age has brought to help them reach their full potential—was not even imagined in my day. In fact, it was just a dream even ten years ago. The U.S. Olympic Committee made it a reality in 1977.

Until recently, an athlete's chance of realizing the Olympic dream was directly related to his or her ability to seek out training opportunities and coaches and to find financial support. For the most part, it was stubborn drive and a great deal of self-sacrifice that brought these competitors to the threshold of the Olympic and Pan American Games. We shall never know how many truly superior athletes in this country missed their opportunity for Olympic greatness because they did not have the wherewithal to make the most of their God-given, natural athletic talents. Through our work here at the Olympic Complex and our attempts to reach out to athletes across America, we are trying to change all that. An aggressive program begun just five years ago holds great promise in helping us reach our objective: to put the Olympic dream within the reach of every amateur athlete in America who has the drive, the ambition, and the talent to "go for it."

The opening of the United States Olympic Training Center in 1977 and the move of the United States Olympic Committee from its New York City offices to the Olympic Complex the following year catapulted the Olympic movement in this country into a new era. The Amateur Sports Act, enacted by the U.S. Congress in 1978, coincided with the new direction and bold efforts that the Olympic Committee was taking on behalf of the nation's Olympic hopefuls. This legislation recognized the USOC as the sole coordinating body for the development of Olympic and Pan American sports in this country.

While the support of the federal government is essential to the future of the Olympic movement in America, it should be remembered that the United States Olympic Committee is not a government organization. Unlike the national Olympic committees of the other 151 nations and territories charged with the responsibility of supervising and supporting the athletes who participate in Olympic competition, the USOC receives no continuing subsidy from the government to support the national Olympic development effort. The Olympic movement in the United States is a uniquely independent effort, as I think it should be. The funding to sustain greatly expanded Olympic developmental programs for the nation's amateur athletes comes from the American people, from corporations, businesses, private foundations, and special interest groups who recognize the value of amateur sports competition in human development. These are people who understand and value the principles upon which the world Olympic movement is founded.

Every American who shares the thrill of watching our athletes compete and, in many cases, win medals at the Olympics shares a responsibility of continuing, sustained financial support. This responsibility extends not only to those who eventually win those relatively few spots on our Olympic teams, but to everyone who believes in the value of international sports competition, and sees the beauty in the triumph of individual athletic excellence. If American athletes are to continue to compete on a par with the athletes of other nations supported in varying degrees by their governments, then aggressive, continued support from the American people and our government is essential. The Olympics are designed as a competition among the best athletes of the world and should remain outside the realm of international politics, but it is our responsibility to send the best prepared athletes we can to this remarkable event.

While the United States Olympic Committee neither seeks nor wants federal subsidies to support the programs it runs for the nation's amateur athletes, the support of the White House and the Congress in a moral and participatory sense is essential. Periodically, important pieces of legislation, which must be reviewed and acted upon by the Congress, are introduced to provide the means through which the American people can contribute to the national Olympic effort. For example, such legislation included the Olympic Coin Act of 1982, which authorized the minting of coins for public purchase to help the USOC meet its 77.1 million dollar budget for the period ending at the close of 1984, and to help finance the 1984 Olympic Games in Los Angeles. An even more important piece of legislation would authorize an income tax checkoff, wherein individuals filing federal and state income tax returns can donate a portion of the refund to the national Olympic effort. Such legislation needs the enthusiastic support of the Congress, the White House, and the American people.

Having served four terms in the Congress of the United

States, my views concerning the value of the Olympic Games and the issues surrounding them do not merely reflect my attitudes and experiences as an Olympian. Rather, my Olympic experience and, later, my service in the Congress, have brought into clearer focus the true benefits of Olympic competition among the youth of the world. Critics and cynics are quick to say that the Olympic movement has outgrown itself, that it has become too political. While it is true that politics have plagued the Olympic movement throughout history and, in fact, were among the contributing factors that brought about the demise of the games in ancient times, the modern event still stands as a triumph to the youth of the world. It is through the determination and dedication of young people and the work of the national Olympic committees that represent them that the Olympics are stronger today than ever. They continue to grow and still exert a unifying and positive influence throughout the world.

Those for whom the Games were intended, the world's youth, remain dedicated to the ideals of sportmanship and fair play. Almost without exception, their ambition is to have the opportunity to compete fairly and equitably with the best athletes the world can provide in their respective sports. For them, it is the test of individual against individual; not nation against nation. It is regretable that certain misguided individuals, politically motivated groups, and governments would wish to interfere. It is from these fringe areas that the politicization of the Games occurs. Hitler's racism in 1936, the riots in Mexico City in 1968, and the brutal massacre of Israeli athletes at the Munich Olympics in 1972 are examples never to be forgotten. But, the Olympics have survived these tragedies, including two world wars, and may, in the future, be the only forum left wherein peoples of the world can come together peacefully and positively, despite political and ideological differences.

As I write these final words, I find it embarrassing to admit that the United States has had as much to do with the non-violent politicization of the Games as any other nation in Olympic history. The decision not to participate in the 1980 Games in Moscow was, in my opinion, a tragic one. While my personal sense of outrage at the invasion of Afghanistan was no less than anyone else's, I cannot agree that depriving our athletes of a lifelong ambition was a proper approach for our government to take. While recognizing that the ultimate decision was with the United States Olympic Committee, it could make no other decision in light of the extreme pressures placed upon it by the Administration and the Congress during that time. The boycott accomplished nothing, deprived basic rights of a select segment of the population, and made sacrificial lambs out of many to whom this nation will turn for its future leadership. As this is written, the Soviets are still in Afghanistan, with forces exceeding that number involved in the invasion in December 1979. World organizations have been powerless to exert any influence to have the Soviet troops removed and, sadly, a group of athletes in this and a few other countries paid a price that was quickly forgotten.

All this notwithstanding, the Olympic movement has survived a difficult time and is once again flourishing. Because it belongs to the youth of the world who will determine the future of mankind and the world's ultimate destiny, I predict the movement will continue to flourish. I am exceedingly proud to be part of it.

Bob Mathias
Colorado Springs